The Wonders of the World and Word

[Berg's] short essays provide an insightful perspective on Scripture and the world around us. They stimulate our thinking and understanding to integrate our worldview with our Christian view. His writings are clear, concise, and cover a wide range of topics.

-JOHN KEOKER, PROFESSOR, FULLER SEMINARY

I always read Myles' essays as soon as they appear. He provocatively assembles his storehouse of knowledge. I find myself saying, "Could that be right?" He loves challenging his readers.

-GERRY ANDEEN, ENGINEER, ASME FELLOW
FORMER MENLO PARK MAYOR

All Christians, at times, reflect on the comparisons and reconciliations between the everyday world and God's Word. It has been an unexpectedly rewarding and enlightening experience for me to share and compare the author's reflections on everyday issues with my own, particularly given his Silicon Valley profile. As I read Wonders of the World and Word, I often wonder if I am looking through the window or a mirror.

-HERB LECHNER, SILICON VALLEY ENTREPRENEUR

COVER PHOTO: The Great Nebula in the Orion Constellation, M42, NGC1976. Generally considered the finest example of a diffuse nebula and one of the most wonderfully beautiful nebulas in the night sky. The distance is between 1,600 and 1,900 light years with a diameter of about 30 light years, or more than 20,000 times the diameter of our solar system.

COVER PHOTO TAKEN BY MYLES BERG, with a Meade LX200 10 inch Schmidt-Cassegrain telescope, using a SBIG ST-8E digital camera and CFW-8 color wheel, using 120 seconds integration for red and green and 160 seconds for blue, on the evening of December 30, 2000.

THE WONDERS *of* THE WORLD AND WORD

101 REFLECTIONS ON THE MEANING OF LIFE

MYLES R. BERG

Guardian BOOKS

Belleville, Ontario, Canada

The Wonders of the World and Word
Copyright © 2003, Myles R. Berg

Definitions taken from *Webster's Ninth New Collegiate Dicitonary*, Springfield, Massachusetts: Merriam-Webster Inc., 1986. All synonyms taken from *Roget's Super Thesaurus*. Marc McCutcheon. 2nd edition, 1998.

National Library of Canada Cataloguing in Publication

Berg, Myles R. (Myles Renver), 1932-
    The wonders of the world and the Word : 101 reflections on the meaning of life / Myles R. Berg.

Includes index.
ISBN 1-55306-453-4

    1. Bible and science. I. Title.

BL240.3.B47 2003 261.5'5 C2002-905974-7

Table of Contents

Foreword

Why write a book? There are more books being written now than ever before and they are all different; each written for different reasons. My reason for writing is to reflect on life. What is it all about, does it have a purpose and, if so, what is the meaning? Socrates, 469-399 B.C., wrote, "A life unexamined is a life not worth living." The evaluation of my life is the essence of my writing. This book is full of thoughts to pass along to fellow travelers on the road of life. They should be considered my opinion at the time of writing, for when I reread them, I know I would do it slightly differently today.

This collection of writings represents the latest set, since I began writing at retirement in January 1992, those from January to December 2001. The basic theme of all the writings is a comparison of God's two creations—the creation of the Universe, our World and all living creatures including humans, and The Word, our Bible. The point of the writings is to bring the World and the Word together synergistically from a wide range of perspectives to stimulate our thinking and have a better understanding. I do not believe we can separate the Word from the World, nor do I believe we can separate the Church from the State. In both cases these are separate entities, but significantly interconnected. It is to our peril that we separate them and deny any interactions.

It is not my intent to persuade readers that these are the only possible interpretations of the meaning of life; instead , I wish to open our minds to possibilities, and develop a process of evaluating each experience in our lives. If there is one pervasive theme, it is that life does have meaning and we need to determine it for ourselves and not let someone do it for us.

I do believe that God has had His powerful hand guiding my life, including these writings. I pray that these may be a blessing to you.

My background is in science and engineering with over thirty-five years of experience in research and development of advanced systems for commercial and military applications. I continue to study the Bible with the same fervor that I do the present unfolding of new discoveries in science, astronomy and cosmology.

> The scientist who lives laborious days in the disinterested pursuit of truth, the artist who will starve in a garret if only he may express the beauty he has seen, the martyr who will obey God in the scorn of consequence, are all religious men or, at least, are men who illustrate that principle which lies behind religion. Truth, Beauty, Goodness—these are sacred, the object of man's true love and

reverence. He to whom nothing is sacred, all questions are open, and the distinction between right and wrong is blurred, is an enslaved, not an emancipated, spirit.

Nathaniel Micklem, *The Theology of Politics* [1941]

Introduction

This book is a collection of essays for which I have not found a way to assemble in a smooth flowing order, but I have separated them into five general classes of similar orientations. The first section is a collection of writings related to my reflections on various experiences. In each case, I relate them to a Biblical understanding. The first section is based on my experiences in life through some sixty-nine years of observing people and the world around us. It is hard to believe where all that time has gone, and if I do not write it down for the next generation it will be lost forever.

The second section is a collection of general observations on the philosophy of life, again with Biblical conclusions. This section is a philosophical reflection on the world around us and its theological significance. It makes an interesting comparison between the worldview and the Christian view. There is a wide range of subjects that were triggered by events of the year.

The third section is focused on theological considerations of God and His creation. What do the Scriptures tell us? The third section is a pondering of theology. Do we understand the Bible? What does the Scripture mean for our lives? Each person must evaluate God's Word for himself or herself and apply it in their lives. This is something that cannot be done for us.

The fourth section is from my background and interests in science. What does science tell us about God and His creation? This section uses my personal background in my career as an engineer-scientist, as a beginning point for the search of meaning. Since my life has had a number of different specializations, this may be of more interest to some with a technical background.

Lastly, the fifth section is a short exercise in playing with words, again with theological focus. This section tries to have some fun with the English language, while still comparing the worldview with the spiritual view.

The groupings are a bit overlapping and ambiguous but some order is essential to help the reader. Each paper is self-contained and independent; however, there may be several in a series examining the subject from a different perspective. The overall perspective is from the Judeo-Christian belief in God.

The appendix gives a listing of all of my writings in 2001. They are not all of equal interest to everyone as each person has their own interests. This list allows selection of essays. I have found that what I think is most interesting does not necessarily match what others think. Therefore, I have not picked and chosen "my best" but have included them all.

I must give credit to the Holy Spirit for much of the inspiration behind all these writings. Without His guidance and encouragement, I would not have made it this far. Special thanks to Angela Boren and my wife Carol for help in editing, and to Lauraine Snelling, Ethel Herr, Hal Hostertler, Pam Chun, Robin Faisant, Rick Langeloh, Gerry Andeen, Berry Wilbanks, Morry Sorrels, George Trete and many more for encouragement in the compilation of these essays into a book. The Mount Hermon Christian Writers' Conference has provided continuing aid to help focus and improve my writings in an interesting and concise manner.

The end of all my labors has come. All that I have written appears to me as much straw after the things that have been revealed to me.

Thomas Aquinas (1225?–1274)

....

CHAPTER 1

Personal Experience Evaluated

E ach day brings new experiences into our lives. We share those experiences with others around us. Is there a purpose for these experiences? I believe there is a reason for each and every one that God has allowed to come into our lives. For many of us, however, these experiences are just random happenings and do not bring a message because we have not pondered the meaning for these experiences in our lives. This is not to imply that we will be able to resolve the purpose for all these experiences but, over time, their importance in guiding our lives and forming who we are will begin to find meaning.

> The new age cannot live on naturalism or on secularism.
> Life becomes sterile and futile without the depth and
> power which come from participation in eternal realities.
> But this new age cannot any more successfully live on reli-
> gious faiths that are out of harmony with known truth, or

that hang loose in the air, cut apart from the fundamental intellectual culture of the age. The hour has struck for the serious business of rediscovering the foundations, and of interpenetrating all life and thought with the truths and realities of a victorious religious faith.

Rufus Jones (1863–1948)
Christian Faith in a New Age

SEARCHING FOR THE SOURCE ················

When I hear a sound, I generally look around for the source. What made that noise? When I smell an unusual fragrance, I wonder how it got there. When I see light reflecting on the wall or other area, I generally check to see what it came from. And when I come across a river or stream, I wonder where its source is. It just seems so natural to be searching for the source. The search continues today with wondering where a specific word came from—what are its roots—and many more such things. We are a curious people and want to find out, "Why?"

Perhaps this is what lead me into science. Not only did I want to track down the source of things, I also wanted to know why. I must have driven my parents crazy with all my "Why?" questions. This continued into school, and the teacher got to be the one answering, "Why?" Eventually I got a job and then it was the boss I asked the question, "Why?" I got married and we had children; they are now asking me, "Why?" The search for the source goes on and on. Is there ever an end? When will all the questions be answered? When will the source for all ever be known?

Up in Alaska we have been active in gold mining. My wife's family has a long history of tracking down gold. They have always been searching for the source, "The Mother Lode." It has been a very interesting search for the source. We have hired a number of geologists specializing in gold. We have supported work at the University of Alaska in the Mining Department for the search and recovery of gold. The locals refer to this quest as "Gold Fever." But there is just nothing like taking out your pan, working the pay dirt at the stream and finding the gold flakes or perhaps even a small nugget at the bottom of the pan, then wondering where that gold came from. Gold in the natural state all has a different color and character. There is the very fine flower gold, the small flakes, the larger course flakes, the small nuggets, and then the few really big nuggets. This is the world of placer mining. The hard rock mining takes on a whole different search procedure.

It is not a big step from the search for gold to the search for God. After all, He is the source of all that is, that has been and that ever will be. Why shouldn't we be searching for God? If I keep asking, "Why?" I will inevitably end up at God. God is the end of the search for the source. One might ask, "Why not search for God directly?" The problem here is that God exists in the spiritual domain and we live in the physical domain. The only place we can really search is in the physical world. By examining what God has created, we can appreciate, understand and marvel at the awesome power of God. As we search for God, He will reach down and guide our search. One good source in understanding how to search for God is the Bible. It not so much helps with the physical domain, but it does help us to understand the spiritual domain and our search for God. The physical world is for us to search for the source, and the spiritual domain requires us to search by reading God's Word, prayer and meditation. By continually searching and asking, "Why?" we will find God's fingerprints everywhere.

EXPECTING THE UNEXPECTED ··············

I go along expecting each day to be like the previous one. Often, what I expected does occur. (If we follow this pattern, we will be more accurate than the weatherman). But is that really what we want? I don't think so. We all like surprises—the good ones, that is.

This condition of repetition is what I rely upon in my retirement years. I would like each day to be like the previous one. This is because any change in this pattern is generally bad news. Recently I got word that a close and enjoyable friend passed away. But we had just gone out to dinner with him the week before and everything was great! Now there will be that "hole" every time we go by where we use to see him, every time we look at photographs or videos and see him as he use to be. That was not what I expected.

At other times it is the weather; too hot, too cold, or too rainy to do what I had planned. I am not as flexible or adaptable as I use to be to accommodate these random intrusions. It takes conscious effort, time and energy to change. Often my wife gets involved and suggests "the list" of things to be done. As I have nothing better, a few items on her list get done and she is very happy. And now that she is happy, the whole house is happy. Not expected, but enjoyable.

There are the times that God comes along and changes the game plan (or allows the game plan to be changed). There is an accident, an opportunity or a possibility. Action must be taken. It is time to wake-up and not continue in the daze of the daily duties. But would it not be nice to look forward to change, to expect the unexpected? What does it take?

For me, it begins with God, *"And we know that in all things God works for good of those who love him"* (Romans 8:28). If I can believe that the unexpected will work for good then, even though the immediate result may be painful and difficult, the unexpected can be endured while maintaining a positive attitude. If I can believe that my toils, trials and tribulation will help someone else, they can be endured without losing perspective. If the flow of life that slowly reduces our capabilities and requires restructuring our lifestyle can be productive, then all is not lost. But for this to occur, one's perspective must be greater than one's self; it must be beyond self. It is one thing to do something for self; it is another to do something for others; but very special to do something for God. Let us consider this.

If I do things for myself, where is my reward? Is there any point at which self is satisfied and, if so, for how long? Can we imagine thanking ourselves for what we have done for ourselves? This action can be a source of pride; just look at what I have done! Besides, there is no surprise, no unexpected result, no special significance; we just did it for ourselves—end of story.

Next, consider things we do for others. There is an inner satisfaction in helping others even if they do not give us recognition or reward. But it is a difficult thing to help others in a way that does not create dependency, control, obligation or discrimination. It is reassuring to receive recognition for what we have done as long as it does not lead to pride. On the other hand, my mother-in-law was always very concerned about being "beholding" to anyone. If you did something for her, she would always do something to balance it out; she did not want to be in debt to anyone. There is a very sensitive balance in truly helping others.

Now we come to doing things for God. We begin with a large debt to God for all He has done for us. Do we do things for God out of a sense of duty, or out of the joy that He loves us? Many times it is a sense of duty, like being in the military. Occasionally, however, it is out of a loving, joyful feeling. Of being thankful for all the blessings He has sent our way. Sometimes there is order and structure, other times it is spontaneous and free. This is perhaps based on the expected, which produces a duty with order and structure. The unexpected generally produces spontaneous and free form praise and worship of God. If our lives follow the expected path, all is order and structure with duties to perform. But with the unexpected, life is free of form, spontaneous and dependent upon our Lord.

WAR AND PEACE ••••••••••••••

There is a cycle all throughout history: when there is peace, differences grow until war breaks out; when there is a war, it continues until there is a victory and, later, peace. What is it about peace that leads to war, and about war that leads to peace? These would normally be considered opposites and not a natural condition that automatically transitions from one to the other. What is it that is unstable about war and peace?

Regarding war, it would seem quite obvious; one side or the other is killed off or surrenders which brings an end to conflict. Without war, we have peace. Now, when we have peace, people go about doing their own thing, and sooner or later, they come into conflict with those around them. Quite often these conflicts are not resolved to the satisfaction of both sides; inevitably, one is declared the winner and the other the looser. The winner goes away happy, the looser angry. From here, conflict grows. We go from an initial state of unity to a division of many groups. The groups take sides—one combined set of groups having a different viewpoint than the other group set. Each struggles for the power to dominate. A trigger will occur, and both groups will be openly hostile to one another. This cycle seems as natural as birth and death. From the moment we are born, we are constantly fighting against death; eventually death will win. Is there any way out of this violent cycle?

Take a look at the Bible. It all began very peacefully in the Garden of Eden. Then Adam and Eve broke the rules (peace is gone) and they were kicked out of the Garden (God's judgment). Once out of the Garden, Adam and Eve settled down in peace with their new surroundings. However, their children became angry and Cain killed Abel after being warned by God to control his anger. God sent Cain off to a far part of the country. More children were born, there was more division, and violence increased. God again became angry at their actions and planned to wipe them all out. But Noah found favor in God's eyes as being a man of peace and respect for God so, before the Flood, God instructed Noah to build a Ark for his family and many of the animals in the region. After the Flood, Noah and his family, along with the animals, began over again in peace; but peace does not last. And so go the rest of the Old Testament stories—war and peace in an endless cycle. Finally, God sent His Son to show people how to live in peace, how to have peace with God and how to rejoin God's eternal family. But the leaders of Israel rejected Jesus and did not accept Him as the Messiah. They rose up and killed God's Son!

The New Testament continues with conflicts and predictions of more cycles of war and peace. Documented next is the time of God's judgment, a seven-year period of great tribulations, after which Jesus will return to rule the earth with power and justice for a thousand years. As this period comes to an end, there will be a great war between the forces of evil and of good. God will step in and wipe out the forces of evil. Then all time will come to an end and the material elements of our universe pass away. After the Great White Throne judgment, the evil ones will be cast away into torment, and those who love God and His peace, are brought to a new earth and a new Jerusalem for eternal life in peace and love. Those of anger, violence and evil will have been removed forever. In light of all this, what do we summarize from the Bible story?

God is a God of peace, love, mercy, grace, and justice. So where does war come from? Satan planned to take over God's Kingdom, but he was cast down with a third of the angels who followed him. They have been at war with God ever since. Not only that, they have recruited many humans to join their ranks in a rebellion against God. We tend to look at war and peace apart from the cosmic battles between God and Satan. Thus we feel confusion, frustration and dismay at what we see. We are not neutral nor innocent bystanders in this battle. Knowingly or unknowingly we have taken up sides. We are either with God or against God. We are challenged to choose sides. Due to Satan's temptation of Adam and Eve and their Fall, we begin life with a sinful nature, and are thus more aligned with Satan than with God. We must make a conscious decision to depart from sin's control and to depend upon God to change our nature, in order to be accepted on His side of the battle line through our faith and belief in God. Eternal peace will only come after Satan and all his followers are cast into Hell. Heaven will then be a place of eternal joy and peace.

EMOTIONS—OUR WAKE-UP CALL ···············

I do not like emotions, plain and simple. The main reason is that I do not know what to do with them. When they do come along, they get in the way of what I am doing and thinking. They upset my train of thought and work schedule. This applies to my own or other people's emotions. For some people, emotions are their way of life. Without emotions, they do not feel they are alive. I just do not see what they find so important in emotions. The psychologists say our emotions are important signals from our mind and body. They are wake-up calls to get us moving and doing.

The word "emotion" has its root in "motion"; from French it is "to stir up" and from Latin, "to move away or disturb." Our emotions are to disturb us, and they do. Most often we are concerned about quieting our emotions. I use exercise, a hot shower, or a hobby to focus my mind on other things, or, as in the case of the hot shower, to relax the whole body. When my emotions are high, I have to move around and do something. I cannot just sit and do nothing. Now, if I just knew what my emotions were all about or what triggered them, then I could do something constructive with them. Most often, however, I have no idea where, why and how they got there; they just arrived unannounced. God created us with emotions, so there must be a purpose.

Interestingly, there is no direct reference to the use of emotion in the Bible, but there are references for being disturbed. Consider Psalm 42:11:

Why are you downcast, O my soul? Why so disturbed within me? Put your hope in God, for I will yet praise him, my Saviour and my God.

There is little reference under "motion," but "move" provides passages in Acts 17:24,27,28,

The God who made the world and everything in it is the Lord of heavens and earth... God did this so that men would seek him and perhaps reach out for him and find him, though he is not far from each one of us. For in him we live and move and have our being.

Galatians 5:24 states, *"Those who belong to Christ Jesus have crucified the sinful nature with its passions and desires"* which is just after verse 22, *"But the fruit of the Spirit is love, joy, peace, patience, kindness, goodness, faithfulness, gentleness and self-control."* So what do we conclude?

There appear to be two types of emotions: those related to love, joy and faithfulness, which are positive and from God, and those related to temptations, passions and desire, which are negative and from our fallen nature, or Satan. God can use our emotions to call us back to Him, for it is in Him we live and move and have our being. But Satan also can use our emotions, to call us away from God into selfish and evil ways of life and being. We must be constantly on our guard and test our emotions to find the source.

LIFE OR DEATH DECISIONS ················

I have seen others, including close friends and family, having to make life or death decisions. For some there is time to make a careful decision after studying all the alternatives. For others, it is a matter of a split-second action. Sometimes these decisions affect others and sometimes they directly affect our lives. What do we do? What can we do?

For me, a major decision-making process transpired in a cardiologist's office in a matter of about five minutes. I had two options. One, do nothing for a month while my cardiologist was on vacation, or do an emergency angiogram with decisions of related surgery determined from these results. As I am very big on procrastination, my preferred solution was to wait. However, my wife and the doctor were very concerned about the possibility of a major heart attack if I waited. And, if there was a heart attack, the damage would already have been done, and recovery operations are limited, assuming that I did live through the heart attack. If I went ahead with the immediate angiogram and surgery, I would have the best chances for survival. My wife was most concerned about the uncertainty and anxiety if we waited so, for her sake I decided on the immediate angiogram and related surgery. I had had an angiogram before, and it was a very unpleasant experience and painful recovery. If surgery was called for, which looked like the logical outcome, there were good chances for survival, but also significant risks of death. This was on a Wednesday and the operation would be Friday morning, but because of the high risk of heart attack, the doctor wanted me in the hospital on Thursday, in order to reduce the risks. So, there I was. How does one handle the burden of life or death decisions? They can tear one to pieces.

The only way I know is to turn them all over to God. I let God decide what would happen and what would get done; be it life or death, the situation was in His hands. I also prayed for the doctors and surgeons for guidance and wisdom in what to do. With that came a peace and quiet so I could get ready for the hospital and all the changes to be made at home. This was a major interruption in our summer plans. The decisions were made as all the alternatives were exhausted. We had to simply rely on God's strength to carry on, whatever was to transpire.

My last chance was on Friday morning, as I was wheeled down to the prep-rooms for the angiogram procedure. Fortunately all was calm and relaxed; what was to be, would be. I remember very little after I was wheeled into the angiogram operating room. Afterwards, there were comments about an emergency triple by-pass as soon as the heart surgery team could be assembled. My wife was there to reassure me. A number of nurses and doctors came by for the various preparation procedures. Then the anesthesiologist came in and started his procedures. Very quickly all consciousness was gone. Would I wake up again dead or alive?

The next vague memory I have was of a nurse asking me what day it was. I had no idea, or if I was alive or dead. She said, "Sunday afternoon." My first thought was, "I missed church this morning." Then all disappeared into murky darkness.

This state of semi-consciousness went on for a day or two. The pain killers and all the other medicines left my conscious mind confused, in a state of hallucinations. If I opened my eyes I saw one thing, if I closed my eyes I saw another scene just as clear and just as bright. Where was reality? Finally after another two days, consciousness was more normal and I could at least recognize people who came by, family, friends and staff. However, I was still plagued with separating the real from the unreal. The unreal seemed so real, but also it was weird, distorted and sinister. I wanted it to be gone. The pain was more endurable than the hallucinations.

Was I alive or was I dead? I did not know for a number of days because my perceived reality was constantly changing. I was experiencing vivid and wild scenes. It was disturbing not to be able to find reality. It was quite a number of hours later that I pondered the nurse's statement of, "Sunday afternoon." This meant that the operation was over and I was still alive. Praise the Lord! From my point of view, being separated from friends and family and enduring these wild hallucinations would be equivalent to being in Hell. The peace and joy along with the presence of family and friends would be heaven.

BRUISED, BATTERED AND BLUDGEONED
BUT STILL ALIVE ················

It was not long ago that I was in the hospital, in intensive care, monitored twenty-four hours a day, with a body that more resembled the dead than alive. There were very few spots left on my body without cuts, scratches, abrasions, bandages and black and blue regions, and that was only from the outside viewpoint. Inside, it seemed that everything hurt intensely even though I was on high doses of powerful hallucinogenic pain killers. Fortunately, I was totally unconscious for the first forty-eight hours of this adventure, then on heavy pain medications for the next week. How does anyone survive such an ordeal? What incredible resilience the human body must have!

I am now home for a period they call "rest and recuperation." From the short term perspective of day to day, which is now how I live, I find very little rest or recuperation. The parting comments from the hospital were, "Cheer up! In another four to six months you should be just as good as new. However, be sure and stay on the program we have given you." Off I went in a wheelchair to be driven home. Home was nice, but it was not the twenty-four hour service of the hospital. My wife and I worked out a routine, which is working quite well when viewed from survival conditions. The progress of improvements in the body is painful and slow. There is still no way I can put on shoes, even the biggest ones I have. But I have hopes, for one day this swelling will end.

How did I get myself in such a predicament? If this were a "normal" incident, we would have called the police and someone would be in jail awaiting trial and sentencing. Who ever did this to my body should pay! Well, it turns out, in one way or another, it is all my fault. I am the one who gave the doctors permission for the heart by-pass surgery. One quick look at my heart with the angiogram and the doctors had an immediate schedule for bypass surgery that noon. This was not something that could wait. I could have rejected the bypass and gone home and had my heart attack all by myself. Of course, they very strongly objected to this option since significant heart damage or death could result. Catching the problems beforehand can provide almost full recovery. After a heart attack, there is much less they can do for recovery. I did buy their argument, but now I am waiting impatiently for all the improvements they talked about.

I believe we all face the same problem when we come to Jesus Christ. We are faced with certain eternal death if we do not agree to permit Him to perform surgery on our body, soul and spirit. The surgery He performs does have its serious, painful and slow healing results. Christ wants to change me, but I am basically resistant to change. Given the alternatives, I do not see any other way to salvation than the one provided by Jesus Christ. There are great testimonies throughout history which support His claim as the Master Physician for our body, soul and spirit.

Christ's recovery room is His church, the body of believers. As we gather together through service, compassion and prayer, we are lifted up with spiritual medicine. Jesus' work is generally not the instantaneous miracles where all is fixed in a flash, but, rather, they involve a slow, continuing step-by-step process which lasts the rest of our lives. It is not until physical death that we pass through to our eternal bodies and where all tears, suffering and death no longer prevail.

The Scriptures reinforce these conclusions:

I praise you because I am fearfully and wonderfully made (Psalm 139:14).

Jesus went through all the towns and villages, teaching in their synagogues, preaching the good news of the kingdom and healing every disease and sickness (Matthew 9:35).

You may ask me for anything in my name, and I will do it (John 14:14).

Salvation is found in no one else, for there is no other name under heaven given to men by which we must be saved (Acts 4:12).

ENDURING THE HEALING PROCESS ·············

I had my heart operation over three weeks ago and I am still very limited in what I can do. The doctors said, "Cheer up, you should be back to normal in four to six months." But that seems like a long, long time. I used to walk briskly at 3.5 mph, but now I am still at a 0.7 mph shuffle. I used to be hungry, eat a lot, but not gain weight. At present I am not hungry, eating about half of what I use to and am still losing weight. I had great ambitions of what I would do during recovery; all of those projects that I had saved up for the rainy day. But my energy and enthusiasm runs out after a little while. There is all this time that just seems to be wasted, with no real progress on either the health front or the project side. What is one to do? What is this healing process all about?

We are very fortunate that our bodies have healing abilities. This is unique, as most all physical devices and structures do not have any healing abilities at all. Once broken, they are broken until someone fixes them. All life forms have limited degrees of healing, which is phenomenal. Life itself is a miracle; the healing process just enhances the uniqueness of life. With all this recognized, why does healing take so long? The older we get, the longer it takes. Why isn't the healing process faster? Is there any reason or logic behind slow healing?

When I read through the Bible, especially the part in the New Testament where Jesus healed, I notice His healing was mostly instantaneous. The people healed were sick, blind, crippled or whatever, and the next moment they picked up their bed and walked away. Now that was some real healing. So, why does it not happen all the time? Why the waiting while healing takes place? Is there a purpose or reason for slow healing, and how do we adjust to enduring the long wait?

There are a number of possible answers.

First, if healing were instantaneous, then there would be no concern about being careful, considerate or compassionate. If there was an accident, people would just get up and walk away. For serious illnesses, the serious part would no longer be present, as getting sick and getting well would occur very quickly. It would be like cartoon characters. In other words, there would be no crying, pain or suffering. For now, however, that is reserved for God's children when they get to Heaven.

Second, there is the reality that we are fallen people living in a fallen world. When Adam and Eve disregarded God's commandment, they were cast out of the Garden of Eden and they were forced to endure toil, pain and suffering. Thus the world environment changed to one of being hostile to life. I therefore relate waiting for healing to be one of the changes due to the Fall.

Third, we are sinners. All have come short of the perfection God requires of us. We do not do the right thing at the right time in the right way. That is a sin because we miss God's mark for our lives. There are potential physical manifestations from our sins, so there is often more than physical healing required. We must receive spiritual healing for our sins, as well. Jesus, when healing a cripple, asked the Pharisees which was more difficult, forgiving sin or healing the body.

Fourth, slow healing gives us an opportunity to evaluate our lives and our lifestyles. For a period in time, the daily routine has been stopped. We have very little to do other than review our lives. We have time to communicate with family and friends. It is also a time when those close to us come by with encouragement and love. They are with us to help us endure the time of healing. It renews one's self worth and the value of family and friends. It opens us up to accepting help from others and being more compassionate in giving help to those in need.

Fifth, the long healing process reveals to us the fragility of life. Life is not something we can take for granted. It does have its beginnings and its endings and, in between, ups and downs. Life is a precious commodity we dare not waste. We can never be sure of tomorrow and what it may bring. Thus, we need to live for each day and make the most of it, whether healing or healthy.

Therefore how now shall we live? It is a time to be open to God's leading. It is also a time when our defenses are down. We need to rely on the help and guidance of others. It is a time to come close to those we love and to share our concerns, our pains, and our dreams. It is a time to review the meaning of life, our goals and the future.

ARE WE READY FOR THE TEST? ···············

When we were going to school, there were always tests. The teacher wanted to find out if we were learning the material being taught or just sitting there fat, dumb and happy. The announced tests allowed time to study and catch up. We put in the extra time to get ready, polish off the rough edges and refresh our memory. But the times I most dreaded were the pop quizzes. We would walk into the room sit down and the teacher would say, "Take out a piece of paper. We are having a quiz today." All the thoughts of what I had passed over casually, left for later to review, and things I had not resolved, popped to the surface. Then came the teacher's questions, all ten of them. "Now pass your papers forward and I will correct them and pass them out tomorrow." There was no place to hide, there were no excuses to give, and no where to run. What was going to happen? On tests I generally did better then I thought. After class we would compare answers and discuss the unfairness of the whole thing.

In life we face many tests. Some we can see coming and others just happen without announcement. Perhaps some simple examples would help. Having to file for income tax comes well announced, but it is still a struggle to get all the information together and turn in our answers. Often we do not get back a grade from the government unless they send out one of their "You Failed" notices. And then we panic. On the unexpected side there are the bad accidents such as automobile, natural disaster, or sudden serious illness. Are we prepared? In these cases, insurance, friends, built-up resources, and internal strength help us to go though the ordeal. For some of these tests of life we cannot be fully prepared within our own resources. What do we do?

We call out for help from family, friends, social groups, and government. Someone must be out there who can help us. If we can just make our needs known, surely someone somewhere will come around and help us out of our disaster. Fortunately, our country has a well-developed social support system. However, it can only do so much with so many in need. Also, there are many areas where no human abilities and strengths are sufficient to restore what has happened. What has happened has happened, and all that can be done has been done. So *now* what do we do?

For those who believe in God, there is a higher resource who is all-powerful, all-knowing and unlimited in resources and abilities. But have we developed the faith to trust and follow His guidance? Is our faith adequate to the test we are facing? Is our knowledge of God sufficient to be assured that He can and will handle our problems? Are His words so engrained in our mind that we can focus on them and not the circumstances that surround us? Oh, those are hard test questions, but they are coming to each and every one of us. Are we ready?

I am writing this in the midst of such a test. I had a number of major heart problems this last week. I read over the American Heart Association's list of most common and less common heart attack warning signs; I have had most of them, seven of the eight. I was able to immediately take my nitro pills, which dilate the blood vessels in the heart, to rest and relax, and to pray as hard as I could with the result that these symptoms pass away in a few minutes. I was back to "normal" but very tired. At the time these things happened I was up at our summer cabin in the mountains with very little medical help in the area. We are now back home and today I go into my cardiologist to find out about my heart test score. I am not sure how he will grade my answer sheet. But I have more faith in how God will carry me through the test. Through e-mail I was able to send out requests for prayers; we are not left alone to face the tests of life, God is always with us. I do not have all the answers, but faith, trust, belief, prayer and God's Word will get us through the tests of life.

Are you ready for the test?

THE HIDDEN PASSAGEWAY ••••••••••••••

I have always been intrigued by the secret doors I have seen in various houses. Typically they lead into a basement area or a storage vault. Most mystery shows involving a haunted house will have secret passageways leading from room to room. It makes for instant surprises. Then, of course, there are prisoners who secretly dig passageways out of prison. They are often caught, but a number have escaped this way. I also think of C. S. Lewis' books in which there was a secret passageway to Narnia in a back closet. What a delightful way to begin a story.

I have always worked for companies with secret and top secret areas behind closed doors. One could not go through these passageways without having special access approvals. I found it very exciting each time I got new special access and could enter the forbidden areas. Some of these excursions included such places as the CIA and NSA, with all of their mystery. There still is something very challenging and intriguing about hidden passageways.

In quantum mechanics and extended fields of chaos and string theory, there is the possibility of "worm holes" that transition between forbidden levels and allow travel over great distances at speeds faster than the speed of light. Generally these passages are used by atomic particles and not humans, but science fiction stories easily overcome these potential limitations. Our minds go wild with such possibilities of these hidden passageways in space.

There is another hidden passageway that few find, but is widely available to those who are searching. This is the mysterious and hidden passageway to God revealed through Scripture.

Enter through the narrow gate. For wide is the gate and broad is the road that leads to destruction, and many enter through it. But small is the gate and narrow the road that leads to life, and only a few find it (Matthew 7:13).

The way to life and salvation is through the narrow doorway.

He said to them, "Make every effort to enter through the narrow door, because many, I tell you, will try to enter and will not be able to. Once the owner of the house gets up and closes the door, you will stand outside knocking and pleading. 'Sir, open the door for us.' But he will answer, 'I don't know you or where you come from.' Then you will say, 'We ate and drank with you, and you taught in our streets.' But he will reply, 'I don't know you or where you come from. Away from me, all you evil-doers!'" (Luke 13:24).

The door is open while we are alive and closes at our physical death.

Jesus answered, "I am the way and the truth and the life. No one comes to the Father except through me" (John 14:6).

Jesus is the door to the Father, salvation and eternal life.

As for you, you were dead in your transgressions and sins, in which you used to live when you followed the ways of this world and of the ruler of the kingdom of the air, the spirit who is now at work in those who are disobedient... But because of his great love for us, God, who is rich in mercy, made us alive with Christ even when we were

*dead in transgressions—it is by grace you have been
saved. And God raised us up with Christ and seated us
with him in the heavenly realms in Christ Jesus, in order
that in the coming ages he might show the incomparable
riches of his grace, expressed in his kindness to us in
Christ Jesus* (Ephesians 2:1–2,4–7).

God is looking for us and wants us to respond to His call
and His love, but only by coming through Jesus Christ.

*Those whom I love I rebuke and discipline. So be earnest,
and repent. Here I am! I stand at the door and knock. If
anyone hears my voice and opens the door, I will come in
and eat with him, and he with me* (Revelation 3:19–20).

God is knocking at our door for us to let Him come in.

*Ask and it will be given to you; seek and you will find;
knock and the door will be opened to you. For everyone
who asks receives; he who seeks finds; and to him who
knocks, the door will be opened* (Matthew 7:7–8).

For those who have accepted God's offer, He will open
the doors.

*And pray for us, too, that God may open a door for our
message, so that we may proclaim the mystery of Christ,
for which I am in chains* (Colossians 4:3).

Paul asks God to open the door of his ministry with the
message of the good news of God's salvation.

*After this I looked, and there before me was a door
standing open in heaven. And the voice I had first
heard speaking to me like a trumpet said, "Come up*

here, and I will show you what must take place after this" (Revelation 4:1).

For John, the door was opened for him to see the future. Let us continue to draw close to Jesus Christ through the mysterious door He has opened. There is no other way. Many follow the broad way of Satan and never find God and salvation.

WHAT TO DO WHEN WE ARE LOST ·············

When I was young I would often go shopping with my mother. All was fine as long as she was in sight. But occasionally I would stop to look at a toy or something else very interesting. Then I lost sight of my mother. There was a bit of frantic searching which of course ended in finding her. Even today I have this phobia about getting lost. I will go shopping on one side of a store and my wife off to the other side. In the process of trying to find her, I generally end up searching the whole store. It is far easier if I say, "I will go out to the car and wait." On tour groups I am concerned about keeping up and not being left behind. There have been a number of interesting episodes on trips we've taken where a few members of our tour group were left behind and they had to somehow catch-up. Being lost is a strange feeling—not one we would want to experience often.

Interestingly enough, when I was a boy scout I had no concerns about getting lost. All I needed was a compass and a map and all was under control. I understood maps and could easily use a compass; there was never a problem. Today there are Global Positional Systems, which further simplify the whole process. However, when I drive in towns and cities without a map, I can easily lose my sense of direction and become completely lost. My wife is the designated navigator and keeps me on track when we are driving. I cannot figure out how or why I can so easily get lost.

Now, if I am lost, I do not like to admit it, and will spend quite a bit of time wandering around trying to find something that looks familiar. If I can just recognize something, then I will be okay. Often I am off searching around for some way back to where I started. My wife has no problem with asking directions when lost. Some how it is just not the manly thing to do.

I can completely understand the Scriptures when they say we are lost and need someone to save us. If I can so easily get lost in this world, which I know, then how much easier is it for me to get lost in the spiritual world, which I do not know? I like the parable about the ninety-nine sheep and the shepherd who went looking for the one that was lost. I associate myself with the lost sheep who wanders off looking at something interesting. It is a great assurance that God pays attention to His lost children and will bring them back home. What does being lost mean in a spiritual sense?

If we do not accept the existence of a spiritual domain, then there is no such thing as being lost spiritually. But here in lies a problem. It is difficult to believe we are in total control of our physical world, and therefore cannot get lost. If we are not in control, it is certainly a possibility that we will become lost. We can lose our sense of direction, purpose or destiny. If we lose these, are we not lost? How can we regain our sense of direction in this world? Our sense of purpose? Our sense of destiny? Can others show us the way we should go? Certainly there are many who want to set our direction, purpose and destiny for us. They claim to be able to save us when we are astray. But how can they do that if they really do not know us and all our appetites, abilities and ambitions? Who can save us when we get lost?

Only someone who is in control of our world and who knows us in great detail can reestablish our direction, purpose and destiny. The only one I know with all these abilities, knowledge and wisdom is God. If we turn to God for our direction, purpose and destiny we will never be lost. But then, we will have to give up our free will of choosing and accept God's will for our lives. Is that worth not being lost? I believe it is.

God's guidance prepares us not only for this world we are in, but also for the spiritual world which is to come after we pass on. God has promised us a place in Heaven to be with Him. He has promised to come and get us and take us back to be with Him forever. For those who do not accept God's guidance, their path for eternity is one of misdirection. They forever wander, and never find a place of belonging, comfort and peace.

THE COMMON, ORDINARY AND FAMILIAR •••••

I am a active member of the "Been There, Done That" club. I am always looking for something new, different and better. How else can we make life active, interesting and exciting? I can't imagine doing the same thing day after day for years on end! I just have to make things different. I am continuously looking for something bigger, better and brighter. If it is a personal relationship, I am looking for someone more creative, exciting and resourceful. Somehow I am never satisfied with what I have and who I know. But this can't go on forever, can it?

When I was young, everything was changing daily. There was no common, ordinary and familiar. However, now that I am much older and retired, the days look much alike. The biggest change from day to day is the weather. If it is cold, I complain about that. If it is hot, that also is a problem. If I get something new, then there is the challenge of figuring out how it works, which is inevitably different then the old item it replaces. If I meet someone new, I wonder if I have the energy, endurance and encouragement to carry on a conversation when my hearing is so bad. I am soon going to give up my membership in the "Been There, Done That" club. I am beginning to really look forward to and enjoy the common, ordinary and familiar. What a change!

There is, however, one area of my life where the common, ordinary and familiar has never entered. That is my relationship with God. He is new, different and challenging each and every day. Because of this, even the old common, ordinary and familiar take on a change as I see them not just from my perspective, but more from His perspective, and that changes everything. Everything is changing, but do we take the time, pay attention and show interest in seeing these changes? The changes are small and not obvious, and we have to search for them. But this is the way we can see God working. Wherever His finger touches, there are changes.

Before recognizing God's handiwork, I was focusing on man's handiwork. I paid no attention to the natural, common and ordinary. They too familiar. Now, however, the man-made handiwork is the common, ordinary and familiar; they are of little interest any more. So it's a big building—someone will build a bigger one. Like the new cars? They seem to get old very fast. Have a beautiful home? In ten to twenty years it will need major maintenance to keep up-to-date. God's creation does not have this problem. No one is going to build a bigger one. Even the old mountains change gracefully into new forms. And the trees and plants multiply and replace themselves as they get old and die. We have a long way to go if we are going to keep up with God.

To keep up with man's world, we have to run real fast these days and use up lots of resources. And what do we get? The need to run faster next time. But with God's world, we have to slow down to enjoy each piece. The joy and pleasures rebuild our strength and endurance. The peace inside our hearts gives rest from all the realities of life. Our soul is refreshed as we commune with God. The slower I go, the more I let the man-made, common, ordinary, and familiar world fly on by so I can grasp the eternal.

WHEN THE INSIGNIFICANT REPLACES THE SIGNIFICANT ∙∙∙∙∙∙∙∙∙∙∙∙∙∙∙

As I look around and listen to people's conversations, watch the TV news and commentaries, or read the newspapers and magazines I find an emphasis on the insignificant at the neglect of the significant. What is so important about the insignificant that it should overwhelm the significant? What is it about reality that we must run away to play games? Where is our focus?

Where might the problem be? Is it in our education and training? Is it in our feelings and passions? Is it in our freedom and pursuit of happiness? Is it in our sense of security and lack of needs? Is it in our search for meaning and importance? Is it in our escape from reality and truth? Is it in our rebellion against God and His absolutes? There seems to be many possibilities!

I have seen many situations degrade from an initial level of significance to the oblivion of insignificance. But, after all, is this not what we see in nature, the entropy and the Second Law of Thermodynamics? All things begin in a state of order, descending into a state of confusion and disorder. Consider our lives; in our young adult years we are full of energy, competing with those around us, and eager to make our mark in the world. Sooner or later, we retire and give all that up to the next generation—we go from significance into insignificance. We go from concern about the nation, our business and family into concerns about our health, comfort, and security. Or consider our creative works, we produce a new, significant, innovative product or artistic piece, only to follow it by work that is similar with small improvements or modifications. It is very hard to maintain a creative, focused, and dedicated significance. It is like trying to remain on the peak of a mountain where all directions lead downward into insignificance. If we do not keep up our diligence, fortitude and concentration, we will be distracted into insignificance.

So, which of the many possibilities in the second paragraph answers the initial question? I believe it can be all of them! Not all at the same time, but from time to time each of those may be the problem that leads us from significance into insignificance. We, including all of creation around us, have a fallen nature. It is not in our natural abilities to remain focused on the significant aspects in our lives. And how might we have succumbed to this fallen state? Certainly not by choice! Ah yes, by choice!

In Scripture we go back to Adam and Eve in the Garden of Eden, where they disregarded God's warning and used their free will when tempted by Satan, the one who is out to deceive and destroy. But let us not put all the blame on Adam and Eve, as often in each day we follow the temptations of Satan and his demons, thus disregarding the warnings and commandments of God our Creator. If we go against the laws of the natural and spiritual domains, what can we expect but to drop from significance into deep insignificance? One may ask, "Is there no relative significance?" That is, a significance based on human values and culture? Yes there is, but since it is relative and changes from person to person, place to place and time to time, of what value is a temporal significance that is here today and gone tomorrow? Today's significance is tomorrow's insignificance! What are we to do?

Only God and His Word are unchanging through all time and space and on into eternity. Now, that is absolute significance! Anything else we pursue may be relatively significant at the time, but rapidly descends into insignificance. I have a house and garage full of things that were once very significant to me, but now are stuff and junk I will eventually throw way. Their value has gone. That which made them important has now changed. So why is it that I still follow the same pattern? I am still tempted by the relative significance of the moment. Why?

We live in the world and find much of our significance in the world, so it is very natural that our worldly temporal things have significance. It is not that material things are bad, as they are in Eastern religions, but that they have a temporal, relative significance. They should direct our attention to the Creator, who is the One with the true significance. Why should we give more attention to the created world than to the Creator of the world? When we replace interests in God with temporal or self-interests we descend from significance to insignificance. It is plain and simple. When our focus is on God, we are ascending to significance, and when not, we are descending into insignificance.

OUR LOST DIMENSIONS OF LIFE ················

There are a number of "things" that affect me which have no basis in physical reality—the four dimensions of space and time. For example, I have been out enjoying a walk in the forest when a cold chill of fear came over me. I had not heard anything, seen anything or felt anything, so where did that come from? Further up the trail I came across fresh bear droppings. Could it have been a "sixth" sense of danger? People had occasionally seen three bears in the area. Then, on other occasions, I have been busily working on a project when suddenly a message flashes across my consciousness about a meeting or telephone call I should be attending to but have forgotten all about. Where did that come from? While touring around the world I have walked into a building and felt a strong feeling about that building, sometimes positive and warm, sometimes negative and cold. Once in my youth I went to see an astrologer with her crystal ball after being encouraged by friends who had done this. They said, "Check her out scientifically." So I did make an appointment and supplied my birth date and birth location. Upon entering her den, I felt a very cold, dark presence as though Satan were there. The hair on the back of my neck stood up; I could feel that! I left with her readings as soon as I could and was glad to be back out in the open space and sunlight. What is this stuff all about? Our lost dimensions of life?

When we think about emotions or feelings, we often describe them as coming from our heart. Or, for severe stress and trauma, the stomach. Actually, neither our heart nor stomach have anything to do with the source of our emotions and feelings. The adrenaline, epinephrine and other

51

hormones released from the endocrine organs into our bodies do effect our heart, stomach and other parts of our anatomy. At other times, we relate these unexplainable happenings to our subconscious, that deep, dark domain of past experiences and connections. For many, there is prayer, meditation and worship to our God. Certainly these are not physical phenomena that the sciences can study, measure and evaluate! But what are they?

In graduate school, I was part of a group studying parapsychology. I represented the physics background for the group formed by one of the psychology professors. He was investigating strange phenomena. We had quite an active group, at least while I was there, reviewing the research of many, including some studies done by SRI for the CIA. (At that time Russia was very actively using psychics for espionage). Also active at that time, NASA conducted some tests with astronauts in space. We interviewed and tested several of the world-famous psychics, which included analyzing their past records. The evidence was overwhelming that there was something of statistical significance happening, but it was highly subjective and not repeatable by standard scientific methods. The mode of communications was not electro-magnetic, acoustic, or gravitational, nor did it show the distance squared attenuation effects of normal physical forces/energy. It is doubtful that the mode of communication is affected by the velocity of light limitations of general physical phenomena. So what is it we are dealing with? Our lost dimensions of life?

In present physics research, our four-dimensional physical world is not enough; present formulations of gravity and other forces require eleventh-dimensional space.

Unfortunately, we have no physical representation for these dimensions. Mathematical topology works fine for any number of dimensions; there are no limitations. However, we are limited in our perceptions and understandings to just four dimensions of space and time. Scriptures note that at the time of The Fall of Adam and Eve, we were cut off from spiritual communications with God. Could this be the source of our lost dimensions of life? Could all these other phenomena be related to a spiritual dimension; perhaps not just spiritual dimensions, but other forms of dimensions, also? We have no physical descriptions or understandings for the "miracles" in the Bible, but they may just be ordinary events in the much larger full-dimensional world we live in, but see, feel and experience only in part. Consider the question of eternity. We are eternal beings. For such to exist, it must exist in dimensions other than our present four, in temporal physical space and time. Yes, even for God to exist and for creation to have happened, there must be more than four dimensions. The case is overwhelming, but can we accept it and the ramifications for our lives?

THINKING, HEARING, SEEING, DOING ··········

This is the way I get things done! First, I have to think about them, then I have to hear about how others have done it, then comes seeing all the details—the actual physical stuff with perhaps someone doing it—and finally comes the doing. My boss at work and my wife at home often will say, "Just do it!" That does not work for me. I have tried that approach and it ends up a most miserable job, both in the doing and in the result. I have to think about the purpose, the objective and the plan. These have to be worked out, even for the smallest of tasks; such as tying shoe laces. I need to hear what others think about the project; what their ideas, desires, approaches and background are. This provides a foundational base with which to work. I have found that without checking with others, I often have an entirely different concept about that which needs to be done. This is followed by seeing all the pieces of the project. I need to develop an image or images. From these I can do the four-dimensional planning in my head—the space and time motion study. Then comes the assembly of all the parts, pieces and tools in the work zone. This can often take longer than doing the actual job. The enjoyment and satisfaction comes after the job is done. I can sit back and relax. The pressure is off. Oh yes, there is the clean-up phase too. It is best not to put off this last step—include it as part of the doing process.

Is this really a practical way to live? We are in the "instant generation." It is the "go, do it!" mentality. Why sit around wasting time with the old-fashioned planning stuff, following the motto: "Plan what you do, and do what you plan!" Why? Because it works! But the time, the time, the time!

So you want an example? Consider Jesus Christ. He had about three years to change the world from the bottom up. He had a plan, a plan His Father gave Him. He was constantly going in prayer to hear what the Father had to say. He kept an eagle-eye out watching what everyone was doing. And then He acted. Direct, efficient, with the resources on hand, and on time. The plan worked.

The problems arise when we see what Jesus has done and we jump in and try to do it right a way, before we have done the preliminaries. We wonder why it does not work. There is a very simple answer: "That is not the way things get done!" There is a process we must endure. In the thinking phase, we must ask, "Is this a project Jesus wants done? Am I the one to do it?" Do we take time to listen to what God has to say to us? It is more important to listen to God than to talk to Him. After all, He already knows what we are going to say! Nevertheless, He wants us to ask. In the asking, I often find that I am not asking for the right thing or asking in the right way. It is an iterative process.

Then comes the seeing. Has God given us a vision of what He wants done? Has God called us to do it, now? I find a lot of waiting after God gives a vision. In one way that is nice. I can begin the planning process. In another way, it is very difficult. I want to do whatever He wants immediately. If God suggests it, I am already out the door and running. Slowly, very slowly, I have learned to wait until He says, "Go!" It reminds me of my early days in track—"On your mark, get ready, go!" Those words seem so far apart in time.

What I have difficulty grasping is the fact that it is not just me doing everything. It is God working through me. All I have to do is to get prepared and be ready (the hard part of the program), and then, when He says, "Go!" I can take off. If I do not do my proper thinking, hearing and seeing, He does not say, "Go." I am not ready yet.

For example, one year I agreed to give train rides to the church preschool children as part of their graduation party. There were about 200 in three groups. That was one of the reasons I built the railroad in the first place. It was an idea God had given me, and He has been actively helping me all along in this project. I thought there was lots of time before the event. But God kept pointing out new things that needed to be done each day to be prepared. It was a rush up until the last few minutes. There was a significant mechanical malfunction, but God took care of that Himself, and no one knew there was a problem. I did not find out about it until the day was over and I was putting the train away for the night. I fixed it before the last group came the next day. Praise the Lord for His help!

WHO'S IN CHARGE OF OUR DREAMWORLD? ···

I have sleep apnea, a condition whereby one stops breathing during their sleep. This is generally not a fatal condition, but it is believed by the doctors and the highway patrol to be a major cause of people falling asleep while driving their car. It can also be a medical cause for one loosing their driver's license.

Because of my heart problems, any further drop in the oxygen level in my blood is consider a dangerous condition. Thus, I have endured a number of clinical sleep disorder analysis sessions. In discussions with professionals, I noticed that it was quite obvious they do not understand all the processes involved in sleep or their purposes. What they do know is the impact from sleep deprivation. The deep sleep phase REM (rapid eye movement) is very important for getting a good night's sleep. This is also the period of time for dreams. It is quite typical that people generally do not remember what they were dreaming when they wake up in the morning. Mystery upon mystery! What is going on in the dreamworld? Who is in charge?

I do not propose to answer all the questions. The psychoanalysts have been working on this for years and have all sorts of theoretical assumptions and answers. What I do want to do is to examine this strange world from a theological perspective. The possibilities are: 1. We are in control. 2. God is in control. 3. Satan is in control. So, let us begin.

First, we conclude that the nightdreamworld is under the influence of our subconscious. (Here, I make a distinction from our daydreamworld, which is generally under our conscious control). Thus, we need to consider our subconscious state and conditions. If there is any natural residing place for our fallen nature, it would most likely be in our subconscious. There are many things stored in our subconscious—as has been determined by hypnotic analysis—all our suppressed emotions, feelings and experiences—real, imaginary and suggested. Also included are probably much of our social group culture; human nature characteristics, morals and ethics, and our gene-based preferences and biases. It can also be proposed that our subconscious is our main connection to the spiritual world. So, what can we conclude from such an open-ended reservoir as our subconscious?

Second, we must propose there is purpose, order and structure to our subconscious, for that is the character and nature of all creation. This does not imply that we understand this structure. It also must be concluded that our subconscious has a significant role to play in our lives. It does have an undetermined, but direct connection with our consciousness. The nature of this exchange is unknown. Now, on to the next steps in this investigation.

Third, what are the major forces that influence us in this world? We think of ourselves, those people around us in various groups, obviously God and His staff, and then last but not least, Satan and his demons. There are a lot of potential sources of influences on our subconscious. I understand people, but what about God and Satan? What do the Scriptures reveal?

Abraham had said his wife was just his sister, so Abimelech, king of Gerar, sent for her.

But God came to Abimelech in a dream one night and said to him, "You are as good as dead because of the woman you have taken; she is a married woman" (Genesis 20:3).

We have Joseph, the great dreamer and interpreter of dreams, given insight by God in Genesis 37–41. The Lord calls Samuel three times at night when he is laying down sleeping. Samuel was afraid to tell Eli the next morning the vision he had that night (1 Samuel 3). The angel of the Lord appeared to Joseph, father of Jesus, several times in dreams given in Matthew 1 and 2. Regarding Jesus, Pilate's wife said, *"Don't have anything to do with that innocent man, for I have suffered a great deal today in a dream because of him"* (Matthew 27:19). From the Prophet Joel, 2:28, on the day of the Lord,

> *And afterwards, I will pour out my Spirit on all people.*
> *Your sons and daughter will prophesy, your old men will*
> *dream dreams, your young men will see visions.*

This is repeated by Peter in Acts 2:17–21, and by Paul, in Ephesians 6:10–18 discussing the armor of God for our spiritual warfare, and the flaming arrows of the evil one. Does this battle take place in our conscious or subconscious minds? Probably in both, but we would need far more protection in our subconscious minds where we do not "see" what is going on! Keep those deceptions, temptations and lies from ever entering our conscious level and having their influences. As for me, I have asked God to take charge of my dreamworld so that I may draw close to Him.

BORN TO MAKE MISTAKES! ···············

As I look back on my life, I keep finding more times I have made errors: I had accidents, forgot to do things, missed appointments, made wild assumptions, made predictions that never happened, under- and over-estimated my abilities, and many, many more things. It feels like I have done more wrong than right! What else can I conclude, except that "I was born to make mistakes!"

Now, life takes on a whole new meaning with this perspective. It extends to accepting that others, also being fully human, were born to make mistakes. Thus, it behooves us to develop a good working philosophy and psychology about how to handle our mistakes and those of others. Now, I did not start off in life believing I was born to make mistakes; no way! My initial position was that "I made no mistakes, I was perfect." Thus, when confronted with the reality and evidence that I had made a mistake, there was great denial, rejection and, if pushed, rationalization and blame on everything and everyone around me. Now, it was not so bad when others made mistakes, after all, they were not as good is I was. If they wanted to do what was right, all they had to do was to ask me and I would tell them! I do not know if you have figured this out or not, but you can get in a whole lot of trouble following this attitude.

I had a number of problems at school with this "being perfect" attitude. How could I explain all the "F"s I received on my English papers? Obviously, the people who devised the English language and spelling were out of their minds, totally irrational, and only trying to make life difficult! My teachers were not persuaded, and insisted their way was right, and mine, wrong. This cost me many hours after school writing on the blackboard. The teachers probably thought they were right in having me do all this extra work, but that was not how I viewed the situation. To me it became a game. How fast could I fill the backboard with chalk marks?

There is a positive side to being perfect. What other people say about you is totally rejected; they are wrong before they even begin. Thus, grades in school are considered arbitrary. Others may consider what I do to be wrong, but I know it is really right because there is a higher reason. This attitude is not a good way to make friends and influence people. I was generally on the sidelines and in back of the crowd. Nevertheless, I was happy, I was right!

It all changed when I met someone who really was perfect and has never made a mistake. I had never seen or met anyone like that. He was totally different. He did not have pride and arrogance in His perfection. He readily accepted all my mistakes and it did not bother Him the way it did my parents, teachers or friends. We could laugh at my mistakes; however, they were still mistakes. He considered them learning steps. I learn much faster making mistakes then by accidentally doing things correctly. As long as I continued to learn and accept my mistakes, He was happy with my progress. I have a very close friend now and we have fun going through the day. I figure I am doing very well when I get things right more than 50% of the time. Of course, that does require asking Him for suggestions and then following the instructions.

I still puzzle over life's creation where we appear to be born to make mistakes. I do learn and grow much faster making mistakes in a loving and accepting environment. In general society, making mistakes is a fast path to rejection, punishment and isolation. Either general society is wrong, making even greater mistakes and not learning from them, or my perfect friend, Jesus Christ, is wrong. I totally believe Jesus is right, true, absolute and perfect. Thus I must also believe general society has accepted Satan's perspective on life, and is out to degrade the life of others as much as possible. That way they look good in their own eyes.

There is a second birth, and we who have followed Jesus Christ will be reborn into perfection. Finally, life will make sense. But the road to eternal life is a very bumpy one and full of mistakes.

THE BOTTOM LINE ••••••••••••••

We were at a Stanford University Business School function recently and heard Charles A. O'Reilly III, Professor of Human Resources Management and Organizational Behavior give a summary of his lasted co-authored book, *Hidden Values: How Companies Achieve Extraordinary Results With Ordinary People.* Prof. O'Reilly's background is in psychology, but he became very interested in business and is now part of the faculty at Stanford. This latest book is based on several years of research on companies which have been far more successful then their competition. What he found is that the extraordinary performance is not only proved by doing things better than the competition, but by doing things completely differently. His conclusions from these studies are that most business schools teach the wrong things; they are not focusing on the bottom line!

We received a short summary of the basic teachings for the MBA—two years compressed into ten minutes—so we would have a background in order to understand what is generally taught and, according to Prof. O'Reilly's research, what should be taught. (This is now part of the standard course work for an MBA at Stanford). The basic factors in sustaining a competitive advantage are: 1. Know what business you are in. 2. Knowing what is your competitive advantage. 3. Functional strategies (success factor, organizational alignment, etc.). 4. Being in the right industry (the growing ones). 5. Being sized for effectiveness. 6. Strong high-technology components. 7. Down-sizing (lean and mean). 8. Going for the high proven talent. Do this better than your competition and you will be better than your competition. Be aware that your competition is also doing these same things; these are the standard MBA procedures. Doing all these things will not give you a big advantage, since everyone else is doing them. To be exceptional, you must do something other companies are not doing, and can't or won't do!

From a human resources perspective, company culture is the central issue. This, however, is not enough. Companies that try to work on company culture generally mix it in with the rest of the MBA structure, but the real challenge is in the execution. Prof. O'Reilly explained the counter-productiveness of mixing human resources with basic MBA teachings in a case-by-case comparison of companies. His "formula" for extraordinary results area: 1. Hire ordinary people, but hire them for attitude and then train them for the skills they need. It is easier to give them skills than change their attitude. Place much emphasis on training. 2. Share company information with everyone, from the top to the bottom. Get everyone involved in the company business. Create a sense of purpose in employees' minds. Build them into a team; teamwork is essential for success. 3. Remove bureaucracy ASAP. It stifles individual and team effort. Everyone is important. 4. Support your workers, and give them what they need. Work needs to be fun. Include families, develop social responsibility—within and outside the company—and maintain high integrity at all levels. Why do you get out of bed in the morning? It should be because you want to come to work!

Most managers cannot or will not execute the above principles consistently. They say they are boring, uncreative, inflexible, illogical; they give many other reasons. The few companies that have been consistent are still growing and expanding market share. It is not easy. Many of the decisions are difficult, and require removing key staff and managers.

I asked Professor O'Reilly a few questions afterwards. I also mentioned that I thought his "discovered" principles seem very parallel to the Judaic-Christian teachings. To which he said, "Yes! Many of the company presidents in this group have a strong religious background and emphasis in their companies." God's principles do work, not only in life, but also in business. I am continually surprised at how many places I see God's hand at work. Who would expect to find God's teachings in the Stanford Business School? God does not demand the credit line or copyright notice on His work. It is up to us to recognize and give Him the glory. By the way, you may want to read Prof. O'Reilly's book, *Hidden Values*.

I CANNOT CHANGE MYSELF! ················

For many, many years I believed there was no problem in being able to change. All I had to do was decide to change and I would do it. It was just that, at those times, I really did not want to change. If I really, really wanted to, I could do it. Now I am at the point where I would like to make some changes to adapt to the aging process and optimize my lifestyle. I find, however, that I cannot change myself! I should get more exercise, but I don't. I should cut back more on desserts, but it just does not happen. I should spend more time relaxing, in meditation and prayer for stress reduction, but I never seem to get around to doing much of that. I want to finish off projects in the garage and at my desk, but the right time never comes. I have been forced to conclude that, as much as I would like to change, I just cannot do it by myself. How can this be?

What I have found are many, many layers of interlocking interests, desires, wants, needs, habits, rationales, philosophies, emotions and passions that formulate and control what I do. To change what I do, I have to go back and alter these basic layers. The problem is that these underlying elements, which have been entrenched for many years, are not easily changed. Changing one is not enough; many or all must be changed. Thus lies the root of our problem. Because of all the interrelationships, there are many side effects of a change we may not desire or want. But change is inevitable!

I had everything going well in retirement; doing all the things I wanted to do and having a grand time. Then it happened. My heart developed problems from clogged arteries. Conditions were such that they could not be corrected by stints or by-pass surgery. They would have to be done the hard way, pills and lifestyle changes. First, I was taking twelve pills a day at very prescribed times throughout the day. Next I had to adapt to the limitations of my heart in the way things could be done: 1. A very slow start in the mornings. 2. A resting period midday, and, 3. A slow-down in the evenings. The cardiologist had very strict rules for what I could and could not do. Of course I test those rules, and many times my heart would respond with angina pain. That required a nitro-glycerin pill and more rest. My ability to change was significantly enhanced by the painful responses from my heart. And that still works today. But there were more changes needed.

Next came a one-week retreat with Dr. Dean Ornish and his medical staff. Everything I did was monitored throughout the day by doctors. Every morning and evening we had meditation and stress reduction classes to get our bodies to relax. Stress is a major factor in heart diseases. Next came the meals and classes on foods and food preparations. We lived on a complete vegetarian diet cooked by an executive chief. The essential is a proper balance. There were exercise classes and, again, doctors monitored throughout the exercise period my heart rate, blood pressure and resulting level of physical exertion. Next were medical classes on heart diseases for one to two hour classes a day. It took this army of professionals to guild and enforce a significant change in lifestyle. There was also group follow-up after the week session. I have now changed my lifestyle, and things are relatively stable at this level. But what might be next?

There is another area I have not been able to change, and that is my spiritual side and my relationship to God. I had been trying to do everything myself, but it was not working.

Finally I asked Jesus Christ to come into my life, take charge and make the changes. He has been working for many years now, changing my lifestyle to match His with the help of His Father and the Holy Spirit. Slowly, ever so slowly, I am changing. Each year a few differences are made. I still do not understand why I cannot make all these changes myself. It seems to require a large ensemble of events, people and God performing a few miracles to make all the changes necessary to become a loving, joyful, patience, kind, good, faithful, gentle, self-controlled person at peace with myself, the world and God (Galatians 5:22–23). There is still quite a way to go, but progress is made daily.

THE STEPS OF REJECTION ⋯⋯⋯⋯⋯

Last week I got news that a cousin had committed suicide. It was quite a shock as he had been part of the family reunions and holiday get-togethers. But Steven seemed to have great difficulties finding his place in life and in the world. At social gatherings, he seemed to be relaxed and having a good time, but there was occasional discussion about him not being able to adapt and, especially, take direction from others; he had to do things his way. There are many who follow their own internal rhythm, their very creative and motivated way of doing great things. Thus, with Steven, his behavior was never considered a serious issue. And then that happened. What might have been going on?

I have never liked anyone telling me what to do. I grew up in a military family. My father was an officer and I was definitely a private or lower rank. There was no option; orders were to be obeyed. I just got used to taking orders. It did not mean that I liked to take orders or enjoyed doing what was commanded, but getting used to them was far better than the alternatives. Throughout my life there always seemed to be someone else in charge—first parents, then teachers, the boss at work, and even my wife with her necessities. Now into retirement, I find that our Lord and God is more present with His agenda. Have you ever tried talking God out of doing something, or reversing that which He has already done? Perhaps the best training I got while growing up was respect for authority and following commands—whether my teachers were right or wrong in my opinion.

The rejection of authority, that is, resenting someone else giving directions, is a very natural human response. This is all part of our nature, our "fallen nature." "I did it my way" was a very popular Frank Sinatra song. Another was "Born Free." We live in a land of "Freedom;" at least that is what all the advertisements say. But that is not what I feel from day to day or year to year. Pressures increase to do things someone else's way. The very natural response is a process of rejection: an attitude of indifference, then a sarcastic comment, followed by deception, where things are changed around just a little, followed by increasing levels of "interpretations," and finally, outright rebellion. It is not a black and white process, but a growing level of rejections. Who is in charge anyway?

We are perhaps missing the real basis in our problem with authority. All these commands are given by God in the Bible. We are to obey our parents, we are to obey those in authority, we are to obey God for, after all, it is His system; He created it and maintains it. He was responsible for who our parents are, He is responsible for those in authority over us, and it is His will for our lives that we are to follow. Until we can come to an understanding and acceptance of God's authority and position in our lives and of those all around us, we will continue to have problems with authority..

I like the way Robert P. Lightner in *The God of the Bible*, summarized our rejection:

> Much of the present dilemma and chaotic condition of both the secular and religious worlds today finds its cause with the setting aside of the "thus saith the Lord" by the clergy. A long series of rejections and subsequent attendant conditions follow the rejections of the Bible as God's Word. Next to that rejection has come the rejection of the God of the Bible. Next, there usually follows a rejection of

the Bible's presentation of man as a lost rebel against God, [and then] comes the rejection of biblical morality and ethics. [After] all of these, the next step is a short one—the rejection of biblical obedience to the laws of God and man. And, of course, many more items of rejection can be added to the list. But the crucial point here is that all of these can be traced back to the initial rejection of the absolute authority of Holy Writ.

The ultimate step of rebellion against others and against God is taking our own life. It is a total and absolute rejection at the cost of one's own life. There is no greater sacrifice we can make in refusing to follow the suggestions, directions, and commandments of others.

THE TRIGGER POINT ················

It was a normal Saturday morning routine, off to Men's Bible study at church. As I was on my way out to the car I saw smoke coming from behind the garage. Not a good sign! I jumped into action; running to get the water hose to see if I could handle the problem or would have to call the fire department. Fortunately it was not too big or serious—my compost pile had caught on fire! Smoke came out of an area about four by eight feet. Although this was not big, putting out the fire was far more difficult than I expected. I hosed down the general area and made sure all was as wet as possible. Most of the smoke subsided and all was under control, so I went back to my routine and off to church.

I enjoy gardening and had developed a good sized compost pile. It was about twenty feet long, twelve feet wide and about five feet tall at the center peak. This represented about six months of raked leaves, grass cuttings and shredded tree and plant cuttings from our one acre lot. After letting the pile sit for about six months, I would spread it around the yard to keep everything fertilized. Meanwhile, the new deposits were going to the second compost pile.

When I got back from church, the smoke was still pouring out of the pile. The fire was burning deep down inside the compost pile. I had put out the surface fire, but not the deep interior. The water hose proved to be ineffective for the deep operation, so I hooked up a big 1 1/2 inch line directly from our well, which can deliver forty gallons per minute at sixty psi. I really went at the compost pile and drowned everything I could reach. This included digging out some of the compost. That would do it for sure!

The more significant changes in our lives generally do not follow a slow, logical progression of reason and thought. There is usually a trigger point that galvanizes action. Most often, these trigger points are not expected nor can they be predicted. For example, consider our decision to accept Jesus Christ as our Lord and Saviour. This was not done by a systematic study of theology or only after a full and analytical review of all the Bible Scriptures. We *may* have done all these things, but in the end it was not logic or reason that brought us to the point of decision. There had to be some trigger point, something that pushed us over the gap of indecision into making a change in our lives. Sometimes the trigger points are very dramatic, such as a fire in our lives and, other times, it is a slow build-up of pressure that finally breaks our resistance. That point of decision is different for everyone. It may come as a challenge, such as Joshua's charge to the tribes of Israel at Shechem:

> *But if serving the Lord seems undesirable to you, then choose for yourselves this day whom you will serve, whether the gods of your forefathers served beyond the River, or the gods of the Amorities, in whose land you are living. But as for me and my household, we will serve the Lord* (Joshua 24:15).

Or it may come as a plea, *"Immediately the boy's father exclaimed, 'I do believe, help me overcome my unbelief!'"* (Mark 9:24). Occasionally, it is very dramatic, as with Saul on the Damascus Road,

> *Suddenly a light from heaven flashed around him. He fell to the ground and heard a voice say to him, "Saul, Saul, why do you persecute me?"* (Acts 9:3–4).

For me, the acceptance of the Lord began very early, perhaps as early as the Long Beach Earthquake, March 10, 1933 when my crib went flying around the room. I was at total peace and enjoying it all. Later on, it was my nightly prayers that gave peace and quiet in facing the unknown of the dark and sleep, knowing that He was in charge. Later in life, my acceptance came through my inability to control everything around me and I turned it all over to the Lord in recommitment. Even today, there is the continuing process of daily turning more and more over to the Lord's control. The less I can do, the more I have to depend on the Lord as my body and mind slow down. Eventually I will have to give it all up as life itself will depart, and accept His gift of eternal life and a home in Heaven as part of God's family. Each step along this path of life so far has had its trigger point; they all have been different. We should look back on the trigger points along our spiritual path and give God the glory for all He has done in our lives.

WHEN IT COMES TO DOLLARS AND SENSE ••••

I heard Professor Douglass North, co-recipient of the 1993 Nobel Memorial Prize in Economic Science, speak on world economics and what makes it work. For perspective, Professor North provided a measure of wealth based on per capita income—the country's gross national product divided by the total number of people. Fifty percent of the world's population earns less than two dollars per day, whereas we receive about seventy-four dollars per day; we are incredibly rich and do not realize it (for family income, multiply by three to four). The frustration element for Professor North is that he knows exactly what it takes to make a country wealthy, but has no idea of how to help a country achieve those conditions. The key elements for economic success are: 1. Property rights. 2. Strong but limited government and 3. Low transaction costs. Perhaps definitions would be helpful, as they were for me. Property rights include physical, financial, intellectual and created property. The strong but limited government requires a government that can and does enforce the laws, commitments, transactions, and secures property rights but does not take over businesses or pursue self-interests of a few over the many—it is a precarious balance. The low transaction costs relate to the cost of doing business—financing, selling, buying, transportation, contracts and legal. For example, computers have significantly reduced the cost of transactions, but the decay of morals and ethics have significantly increased the cost (legal and accounting costs have skyrocketed). The world is not a stable economic system; 1000 years ago China was the most advanced, it is now in the third-world class, but growing. Western Europe was in the dark ages and is now one of the leading powers. In the 1940s Argentina was sixth in the world, then Juan Peron took charge and it rapidly sunk to third-world status. Then there was the recent collapse of USSR from massive economic problems. How do we make sense of the dollars?

Many people have analyzed the "success" of the West, particularly the USA. What is it that has made us so productive and wealthy? We have tried to export the "good life" in many ways. We have movies that travel around the world, government programs to third-world and other countries to try to get them on the "right" path. United Nations also has various support programs to help the needy nations. There is also the World Trade Organization, which promotes free trade and settling grievances between counties. Such work as this has gone on for centuries. But there has been only limited success.

Some relate this success to technology, and many foreign students come to our universities for their bachelor, masters and doctoral degrees to carry the training and technology back to their countries. Certainly technology has been an enabling source for the recent jumps in productivity and whole arrays of new products. Technology has pushed the productivity of people. All this must be included in achieving success. But it has not always worked.

Others have proposed that it is Western religion that leads to the higher morals and ethics which are the underpinnings of a productive society. In this is rolled up human rights, government responsibility and even ecology—proper management of the earth's resources.

Professor North did answer a question from the floor about the role of religion in economic growth. His concern was that they had no way to measure it! There was no direct connection that was pivotal in getting the whole amelioration process going. Religion certainly helps and provides good input to society standards, but it does not necessarily make the needed changes happen.

What do the Scriptures say?

And why do you worry about clothes? See how the lilies of the field grow. They do not labor or spin. Yet I tell you that not even Solomon in all his splendor was dressed like one of these. If that is how God clothes the grass of the field, which is here today and tomorrow is thrown into the fire, will he not much more clothe you, O you of little faith? So do not worry, saying, "What shall we eat?" or "What shall we drink?" or "What shall be wear?" For the pagans run after all these things, and your heavenly Father knows that you need them. But seek first his kingdom and his righteousness, and all these things will be given to you as well (Matthew 6:28–33).

Such reasoning and analysis would never show up in economics theory!

AWAKE, ALERT AND ACTIVE ···············

In the old days, if they had a several days' journey, Yankee fishermen had the problem of delivering cod to market in good condition. The fishermen tried many ways to rectify the problem, but the cod always arrived in poor condition, even through they were put fresh in water tanks and fed. They arrived alive, but when cooked the fish were soft and tasteless. Finally, one adventuresome fisherman put a few predators in with the cod; the cod were always at risk of being eaten. Having the "enemy" present, kept the cod awake, alert and active. When the cod got to market, they were in very good condition and the fisherman got a good price for his catch. Perhaps there is a lesson for us to learn?

We go to a mountain cabin near the source of the Sacramento River. This is a popular area for trout fishermen. In the summer time the Fish and Game Association replenishes the trout from their fish hatchery ponds. When the fish are first put in the river, they are soft and not very flavorful once caught and cooked, but after a few weeks surviving in the wild river they are very tasty and firm. Just being protected and well-fed in the hatchery does not produce good fish. This would seem to be a modern parallel to the above story.

We might picture ourselves "swimming" around in our world. If there were no enemies and the food were plentiful, we too might become drowsy, dull, dormant. Why keep in good shape physically, mentally and spiritually? There is no need! As much as I would like to believe that I could maintain a vigorous lifestyle, I doubt that it will happen. I even have an experience to reinforce this natural relaxed conditions of humankind.

During the Pacific Nuclear Test Series, I was one of the many scientists monitoring the effects of nuclear explosions. As you recall, all the natives living on Eniwetok and Bikini Island were evacuated to other atolls. For one of our measurement programs we used the Wotho Atoll where about fifty natives had been transplanted. Most everything was provided for them, including movies in the evenings; they did not need to work. The only things moving in the mornings were the children off the play. It was around noon before the adults were up and moving. Life was very slow paced. Their big event of the day was watching the movie that evening. It was very easy to fall into this pattern. The challenge was to maintain a strict schedule, which was necessary in order for us to get all our test equipment up and operating and take all the necessary measurements. It would have been so easy to adopt that relaxed lifestyle if there were not something important keeping us going.

Consider the Proverbs: *"Go to the ant, you sluggard; consider its ways and be wise!"* (6:6). *"A sluggard does not plow in season; so at harvest time he looks but finds nothing"* (20:4).

A little sleep, a little slumber, a little folding of the hands to rest—and poverty will come on you like a bandit and scarcity like an armed man (6:10).

I went past the field of the sluggard, past the vineyard of the man who lacks judgment; thorns had come up everywhere, the ground was covered with weeds, and the stone wall was in ruins (24:30–31).

And *"A fool spurns his father's discipline, but whoever heeds correction shows prudence."* (15:5). *"Folly is bound up in the heart of a child, but the rod of discipline will drive it far from him"* (22:15).

79

To retire from life is built into our fallen nature; it is so easy to do nothing, at least, nothing really significant. Can we consider the torment and tribulation in this life as God's gift to keep us strong and healthy? If by nature we become the undisciplined sluggard, what option does He have? Perhaps Satan's role is that of the predator, seeking those he can devour. This does keep us running and seeking God's protection. There are many things in this world that keep us awake, alert and active if we want to stay alive. But why is it so easy to become drowsy, dull and dormant? Is that perhaps Satan and his demons at work tempting us to nothingness? A way to *divert* us from finding God and doing His work on earth, to cause us to lose sight from where our real guidance and strength come from—the true source of all life is God! It is so easy to "waste" God's precious gift of life. Consider Paul's comments in 2 Timothy 4:6–8,

> *For I am already being poured out like a drink offering, and the time has come for my departure. I have fought the good fight, I have finished the race, I have kept the faith. Now there is in store for me the crown of righteousness, which the Lord, the righteous Judge, will award to me on that day—and not only to me, but also to all who have longed for his appearing.*

ENJOYING WHAT OTHERS DO ················

I have great difficulty enjoying what others do in different ways. The first instance is when I can't or don't know how to do whatever it is they're doing. I believe there are two reasons for my discontent. If I cannot do it, there is embarrassment or envy. Why shouldn't I be able to do it? Somehow I am inadequate. It makes me feel small and insignificant. The other factor is not knowing the skill or having the equipment to do it. I feel dumb and uneducated. This again shows my weaknesses. For either of these, there is a comparison; I'm not as good as someone else. I keep hearing that "we" are all equal; but that is not true in many ways. So how can I enjoy what others are doing?

The second concern is when someone does something for me that I can do myself or gives me something extravagant. Here, my feelings are exactly the opposite of the above. I do not feel recognized; I should be doing it or I do not deserve a gift. I feel like they do not consider me capable of taking care of myself or that I'm not independent. I get very embarrassed and frustrated over receiving gifts; I don't feel I deserve their attention. I may also feel obligated because it seems they want something in return. This is the feeling of being used, taken advantage of, or of a hidden commitment. What can I do to enjoy being with others?

From these two instances of not always being able to enjoy what others do, it might be concluded that I am schizophrenic; on one end, I am as good as any anyone else and on the other end I am not worthy of anyone else. What can I do? As a temporary solution I just turn off my feelings and assume it is just a job to be done or a game to be played.

If things do not work out, that is just life. If somehow things work better, it is a pleasant surprise; a bit of luck. It is just a way of surviving on this planet.

There is a hidden source that strives to produce both these instances of discomfort in our lives. This is our long-term enemy, Satan. First he tells us we are like gods, we can be and do anything we want; we can be masters of this world. Who wouldn't like that? However, each time we fail, he is there accusing us of being unworthy or never amounting to anything! It is a giant set-up. First we try to be gods but eventually we fail. Then Satan calls us total failures. And we let him do this to us!

Satan has every advantage over us. He is more intelligent, more powerful, and has a third of the angels following his commands. We are out-numbered and out-gunned; there seems no way to win. He is very subtle and most often we never know we are being attacked. Thus, we are totally under his influence. My dual nature falls right in line with Satan's attacks; the source has been identified! But how can we defend ourselves against such attacks?

Obviously, we have to find someone more powerful and more intelligent than Satan and all his demons. Also, someone who is willing and able to help us. There are not many options. I know of just one. That is God Himself. After all He created Satan and is able to control him. The Holy Scriptures tell us that God has already put limitations on Satan and how far he can go in attacking us. A good thing too, otherwise we would all be dead. It would be no problem for Satan and his group to eliminate all life on earth. Fortunately, God is for us. He created us, loves us and wants to save us. But we must totally accept His strength flowing in our lives. To do this, we must repent of our rebellion against Him and be reborn into His family as His children. This allows us to use the full protection of God. Paul encourages us in Ephesians 6:10–18,

> *Put on the full armor of God, so that when the day of evil comes, you may be able to stand your ground..., the breastplate of righteousness, the gospel of peace, shield of faith, the helmet of salvation, and the sword of the Spirit.*

As for my "schizophrenia," God did not create me "equal" to everyone else, but specially designed me for the purpose He has for my life. As I accept God's plan, all these other feelings go away; I do not have to compare myself to others, nor compete with them. As for accepting what others may do for me, I just have to remember all God has done for me. If I can accept what God is doing in my life, I have no problem enjoying what others are doing in my life. In God, all the missing answers to enjoying life can be found.

OVERWHELMED BY DETAILS ·················

I like to do things in the proper way, by following all the correct processes and procedures. It does take a little longer, but there is more satisfaction in doing things right the first time. Lately, however, the proper processes and procedures have become impossible to follow; they have become complicated and very confusing. As I do a bit of writing, I read over the writers' style manual to be sure I am doing it all correctly. After reading it, I am more confused than before. There are several new trends—one is to reduce the number of capital letters. The new procedure requires attention to the exact use, the desired emphasis and local customs; it may or may not require capitalization. Along with this is a trend to give the writer more freedom in style, punctuation, spacing, and letter size and character to better set forth the mood and feeling; be creative in the style and not follow any set rules. So, what is a struggling writer to do?

Then we come to the dreaded income tax forms and instructions; my next big project. How impossible it is to understand and follow all their rules and regulations, not to mention all the exceptions and special conditions. I have given up trying to understand the tax forms. My solution is to get a computer tax program and just put the information in and let it calculate my taxes. I have no idea what the computer program does with the numbers and the taxes always come out higher than what I expected. Once I talked to several tax specialists and got completely conflicting directions on what to do, so I used the directions with the least tax consequence. But what are we to do when overwhelmed by details?

Next I am reminded of the rules and regulations for various church denominations. What is respectable behavior in one church is a forbidden sin in another. When it comes to how the churches are organized and manage themselves, that, too, is most varied (last count gave 256 different ones). There is the controversy over which Bible translation to use; each congregation seems to have their preferred version (the count here was sixty-six versions available in English). And there are more substantial differences when it comes to interpreting the Bible— some with a literal view, some with a liberal view, some with a focus on selected passages, and some where one wonders if they open the Book and use other sources with equal or higher authority (occasionally referred to as the cults). What are we to do?

Everyone has a different way of adapting to the structure of society. Some are in rebellion from the very beginning. They are free spirits doing what ever feels good. Others see it as playing a game; the only important thing is not to get caught. Most struggle to follow all the rules and regulations—they try hard to stay within the lines, but it is not always possible. There are a few who live and breathe laws— the authority figures who enforce them—somehow they always seem to bubble to the top and find ways to introduce new laws into the system. I can visualize Martin Luther nailing his ninety-five theses on the Wittenberg Castle church door on October 31, 1517, in what began the big Church Reformation. From my perspective, we need more reformations to eliminate being overwhelmed by meaningless details around us.

There is one possible avenue of escape, without having to reform the whole world. Jesus Christ said,

Take my yoke upon you and learn from me, for I am gentle and humble in heart, and you will find rest for your soul. For my yoke is easy and my burden is light (Matthew 11:29–30).

Obviously Christ is the transforming power and is able to do what we can not. We seek our refuge in Him. When we feel overwhelmed, we just pass that all over to Jesus and accept His peace. With His guidance, all our tension, trials and tribulation become manageable.

One might ask, "Since Jesus said, 'My yoke is easy and my burden is light,' how come our Christian churches have made religion such a burden?" The Gospels reveal Jesus reprimanding the religious leaders of His time for laying such heavy burdens on their people. He also had heavy words to say to all those in authority. I think it is time for Jesus to return and give the same message! Jesus promised to come again. So for now, pass our ever-growing burden of overwhelming details on to our Lord Jesus Christ.

CHRISTIANS DON'T HAVE FUN ················

If it isn't unethical, immoral, illegal, discriminatory or dangerous, how can we have any fun? If we watch and listen to the communications media, the humor has sexual overtones, visions of revenge, it denigrates God, humiliates other people, portrays wild binges and other irresponsible activities. It seems that being an upright, honest, law-abiding citizen, concerned about our fellow human beings is labeled hard work, boring and to be avoided at all cost. Consider our "war on drugs," one of the most ineffective programs for changing social patterns. Pornography is one of the largest businesses on the internet. Consider the tremendous increase in gambling; not only in Las Vegas and Reno, but at Indian Reservations and now in many states, with big Lottery programs. There just is no fun in being good. What is going on?

If we ask the media why they broadcast this type of material, their answer is very simple. It makes the money and pays the bills. The popularity ratings are much higher for these types of programs. The illegal drugs, pornography and gambling provide very large profits. Everyone wants to get on the band wagon and make lots of money. Even activities that are proven harmful, such as smoking, produce large profits for their manufactures and promoters. If we look at politics we can see it follows much the same pattern. If it is not based on money and power, it does not get much attention.

One way of looking at all these activities is that people are desperately looking for ways to escape from their day-to-day lives. They have a vision that life must be more than just living the normal, simple life. Everyone is working hard to make more money at the expense of enjoying what they are doing to make this money. Having worked hard with stress and strain to make all this money, what to do with it? Obviously, we spend it! But on what? Whatever will bring us happiness! The only thing the money will buy are things that people can produce. We cannot go out and buy one pound of joy, peace and happiness. But we can go out and buy bigger homes, cars, toys, entertainment and pleasures of all kinds. And somehow believe or hope these will bring us the joy, peace and happiness we really want.

My doctor has a maxim on his wall, "When we are young we spend our health to make our wealth and when we are old we spend our wealth to regain our health." I wish that were not so true for me; I have recently spent a lot of time, effort and money seeing doctors, taking pills and changing my lifestyle to regain some of my health. It would have been far more effective to have changed my lifestyle long ago and therefore not have to put up with all these limitations now in my retirement. I had a number of things I wanted to do upon retirement, but many of those have now been dropped out of necessity. However, back to our discussions about having fun.

I have tried a few of the activities the world calls fun, but I did not have any real fun doing them. There may have been a short burst of excitement and entertainment, but when it was all over, there was nothing left. I would come back to work from a nice vacation, only to have the memories fade quickly away in a few days—where had my vacation fun gone? All I had left were a few pictures and some stories to tell. But things are changing.

I have found the source of joy, peace and happiness and it does not cost a lot of money. It is developing my relationship with God through His Son Jesus Christ. I have been a

Christian for many years, but did not spend much time at it as I was busy making money and supporting a family. Now retired, I have many hours each day that I can devote to expanding my walk with God. In return, this brings boundless joy, peace and happiness, things that money cannot buy. Why is it that we rush off in all other directions looking for the fun of life, neglecting the source? Must be that Satan and his dominion are very effectively working hard to deceive us, including the vision that Christians do not have fun. A relationship with the living God is not seen as fun when the world follows Satan's world of fun, but it is fun as we were created to have. Not a substitute, but the real thing. And we do not have to harm, degrade or kill ourselves to get it. In fact, it is the opposite, we will live a better life with God and be with Him into eternity.

EXCESS BAGGAGE ················

When we get ready to travel, the bags come out and packing begins. What will we need? The bags begin to fill up. On to the next suitcase. Each time I have traveled, there were things I wished I had packed and didn't. So, next time, even more! However, there were all the things I took and never used. Just so much dead weight and space. I had good intentions and lots of planned uses, but just never got around to them. For example, on this present trip to Kauai, I brought a tripod for my camera. I have used the camera a lot, but not yet used the tripod. When we go by car, the problem is far worse—we end up filling the whole car with stuff. Lots of excess baggage.

Now I have the same feeling about going through life. I have all these things and stuff and junk hanging around, getting in the way and requiring attention from time to time. I don't need that! I am trying to cut down on all this excess baggage as I go through life; but I have not been very successful! I have things I have moved from place to place that I used in high school; that was over fifty years ago. One would have thought that, by now, it would all be long gone. The excess baggage is still around.

Then when I examine myself—a dangerous thing to do—I find there, too, are a lot of things I am dragging around as excess baggage. There are old feelings, worries, concerns, memories, a few physical problems and a bit of extra weight all slowing me down. Time is getting more and more precious. I do not have time to pay attention to that excess stuff, but have not been able to get rid of it, and should. I can't just pick it up and stuff it in the trash can, like the physical stuff. Something needs to be done to get rid of all this excess baggage.

I am also concerned about my spiritual baggage. There are a lot of old, past teachings, interpretations and thoughts that limit and block new experiences and hold me back from further growth in faith and trust. I get new, fresh insights in reading the Scriptures and listening to Bible study groups, but I am very slow to grab a hold of these concepts and put them to work. The old saying, "Trust and obey for there is no other way." gets stuck in the conservative, cautious, and careful approach to life's experiences, many things that did not work the way I had expected. It is much harder to change direction with all this excess baggage I carry.

Jesus said, *"Then you will know the truth, and the truth will set you free"* (John 8:32), and *"For My yoke is easy and my burden is light"* (Matthew 11:30), but still I drag behind me all this extra stuff. How can we free ourselves to follow Jesus' truth more fully? Jesus also said, "Give me your burdens." I try this, but often I just take them back again. Jesus also commented to a man who had many things, "Give them away to the poor, and then follow me." I have gotten used to all the things around me and have a difficult time imagining getting rid of them. Many are "just in case" items, saved for special times of need. We are told to be prepared for the big earthquake, there are projects on the thought table that I would like to do, and there are always many fix-it tasks that pop up from time to time—we just need to have the right stuff available to get the job done. Then, there is a whole category of stuff I have not looked at in years and which is just a pain to go through. I save these treasures from the trash, but it must all go. Excess baggage is a continuing problem as each day I collect more.

If I could just put more trust in Jesus Christ as my Lord and Saviour, it would be a lot easier to get rid of all the excess baggage. Once I got rid of it, it would be a lot easier to put my trust in the Lord Jesus. The thoughts of, "May be I should be doing this myself" would not be there, because the stuff to do would not be there to tempt me. If I could get rid of the wants, the shoulds and the would-like-tos of my own making, and put in Christ Jesus' desires for my life, this burden of excess baggage could be easily taken care of. Slowly, through prayer, meditation and Scripture study there are changes taking place. It also helps that as my body grows older, I can do far less, which makes it easier and easier to get rid of the excess baggage. But there is still a long ways to go. The real down-sizing and excess baggage dump is yet to come—consider our transition from earth to Heaven! No need to pack the bags for this trip, all is left behind.

RESTORE, REPAIR, OR REPLACE; THAT IS THE QUESTION? ···············

There is a constant stream of things crossing my workbench that need help. Some are beyond fixing; it is cheaper just to replace them. This is the easiest to do. I prefer this approach because we can get a better item that's more up-to-date. Next comes the fix-it series. If the problem is simple, like a flat tire or a missing bolt, those are quick, simple and all in working order soon. As a result, I feel I have accomplished something and the workshop is moving right along. The last category includes those items which need a lot of work—a major clean up, replacing worn parts, taking out dents and scratches and the full paint job. It is the work of restoration—a much longer process. Even after all the work is done, it is still an antique item. The value is in its age, history and uniqueness. We have many treasures from our parents, grandparents and even great-grandparents. Even a few real ancient items like Wooly Mammoth bones, teeth and a tusk that were taken out of our Alaskan gold mine and from the surrounding area. All are about 25,000 to 35,000 years old. I went through various steps of restoration to keep these from further deterioration.

My thoughts then jumped to God and His workbench, as people and various other things come to Him needing help or are not working right. What does He do—restore, repair or replace? I think of Moses, Abraham, David and many other of the great names in the Bible. I believe God sits back and reminisces about all the things He accomplished through them. They are His treasures. These people he carefully restores. He wants to preserve their nature, characteristics and their lives. He wants them there for all eternity. Next we come to those who were fighting against God; those who follow Satan. For that bunch, I do not believe God wants them around; there are no good memories and many things spoiled because of them. Those I expect He will just throw away; good riddance. They can be replaced by some new ones.

That leaves us with those who come to God for help, seeking His advice, His healing and His blessings in their lives. Some have great faith that God will help them and others have just a very little bit of faith, God is their last hope. These I believe fall into the repair category which may include a little testing and evaluation to help them determine their real needs versus their wants and desires. I conclude this, as God does not always answer my prayers the way I expect. He has a different view of where I need help and where I have gone off in the wrong direction. So He begins His repair work. Sometimes He seems very slow and, other times, He works on a problem I did not even know I had. In the end, it all seems to work better than if I had done it myself. The whole point of God's repair service is to get us aligned with Him and His will. It may be a short process or a long one. How we respond will determine the future direction of our lives and God's continuing repair, restoration, or rejection of our lives. This is a time for growth, either toward God and His love or away from God and turning to our own self-control.

God's repair work is a time of trial, to help us grow into one of His treasures, or for us to rebel and insist on our own way. He does not force anyone to follow His will for their lives, even though that would be the best for them. We come to Him for what we think are the big problems, but He generally sees them as very small. It is more often our problems we do not see that are the big ones He works on. His goal is to help us reach our full potential; that is the way He designed us. Often, however, we continue out of control. In place of doing all the work Himself, He will often send some of His saints or angels to be with us, to help us and to guild us. Thus, we may never know how many different ways God has tried to touch us with His love.

Fortunately God's perspective is not ours. We would generally prefer to replace than repair, and restoration is only left to the professionals at a great cost. We must remember our restoration did cost God the life of His only Son who came to earth as a man and was sacrificed to pay for our sins, so that we could be restored to full relationship to God though our repentance and following of Jesus Christ as our Lord and Saviour. The honor, glory and power belong to our God!

WE ARE MISSING PARTS OF THE PICTURE ·····

I got a new camera recently and I have been taking many pictures. My new camera has some features which make taking pictures fun again. I have noticed, however, that on several occasions I have cut off part of a person or part of a scene. I did not mean to do that. The picture is just not complete. When looking at photographs, it is quite obvious when there is something missing that should be in the scene. And so it is with most of life; we can tell when something is missing.

Consider observing other people as they go about the streets and by-ways of our cities. We notice when an arm or leg is missing. Or if we are watching a building be constructed, we can tell that there are things missing. It is just obvious when there is something lacking. The big things are quite noticeable especially when we are very familiar with what they should look like.

The problem of something missing becomes more difficult when it is not obvious on the outside, or it is an areas where we have no previous experience. I have met several people who have had serious strokes. It may not be obvious in their physical being, but when talking to them or watching them try to do something simple, it is very apparent that something is wrong. And so it is with many things; the longer we study them, the more we find things that are missing.

I have been concerned about our universe and ourselves in particular. From all I have experienced in the past years, I notice we have a very incomplete picture—there are many missing parts. So, what do we do about that? We either make up a story, study further or just forget about it. None of these is a solution, at least, a good solution. In the days of our early culture, we made up stories or explanations based on god-like beings or creatures to fill in the gaps in our picture. But these were only temporary fixes. We now look at them and laugh. Are we doing any better?

As I was growing up, my parents made sure I went to Sunday School. I learned all about God's creation, the big Fall, the coming of Jesus to save the world and then, a bit later, from the Book of Revelation, about the End Times and the New Heaven and New Earth. I have continued studying the Bible and trying to fit all the pieces into the missing elements of the Big Picture. It just is not all there. There are very large pieces missing. For example, "Why did God create the universe and ourselves the way He did?" It does not quite make sense to build something you know you are going to put into the fire and burn up and then start all over again. And His idea for people—two different kinds, men and women. Together they make one—that is, able to produce following generations. Neither one, alone, is complete. More specifically, the Bible states we are not complete unless we are in relationship with God where He is part of us and we are part of Him—we are not fully "one" as husband and wife. The next big problem is eternity; we know life is short, where we see a very small piece of life and the universe. How do we fit a temporal life into an eternal one?

When I continue to read the Bible, the answer I find from God is, "Trust Me, I got it all figured out and ready to go." What this tells me is that there is a major part of the picture of the universe and of life that is missing. In addition, I am not going to find the answers in my lifetime on earth. Further, God states, "There is no one who can challenge me or can change my plans! I control everything; past, present and future. Be at peace and enjoy the ride. But remember to follow my commands so that your life may endure."

It is with fear and trembling that I proceed with life. So far God has been very loving, supporting and guiding through each step of life. However, I am completely dependent upon Him. It is very hard to be at peace and enjoy the ride through life when you feel totally out of control. It is like a roller-coaster ride; we are only able to look back to see where we have been. I just hold on tight, close my eyes and pray God will do all He has said He will do. (Close my eyes? The picture I see looking forward is very fuzzy, confusing and scary). How strong is my trust and faith in God? For one point, I do not have an alternative. For a second, God has always been there when I needed Him. And for a third, He has promised never to leave those who love and follow Him.

OUR WORLDVIEW ••••••••••••••

We all develop a worldview. Some may have not changed it much since childhood, others wait for reality to strike, and still others are constantly testing their worldview with what they see, hear, feel, taste, and sense each and every day. Thus it is not surprising that our worldviews do not agree. As if this were not enough, we have differences in race, gender, language, culture, nature, natural and trained abilities, economic and educational conditions, and many, many more. Thus, given that we all have our own private worldview, so what? These all become major problems when we try to communicate, try to expand relationships, and try to develop societies. How would it be possible for a group to be established unless they had some common worldview in a specific area? How would they ever develop a common language, understanding and points of view? Let us consider an example, a nice, controversial one.

What is our view of God? In very general usage, everyone has their own outlook of God. The problems, controversies and hostilities begin when we try to communicate our beliefs. No one is in agreement. Are we surprised? We shouldn't be. From the many reactions I have had, it seems everyone expects my perception of God to be identical to their view. The general assumption is that everyone is climbing the same ladder, just that some are farther up than others. It is said, "All paths lead to God," but even this assumption has serious problems, as most major religions of the world have different beginnings and different ending points. For someone to say that all religions are the same, is to reveal they have not tested the reality of their worldview in many years. What is this business about reality tests?

For something to be real, true and absolute, it must be tested. Suppose I walked into a bank, said I was Bill Gates and wanted $1,000,000. What would they do? They would go through a lot of testing to determine if I really was Bill Gates and the account with them would support a withdrawal of $1,000,000. If not, they would not be in business very long. We need to be about the same actions with our worldviews, or they also will go out of business—no longer an effective force in our lives. Now back to our view of God. How can we possibly test it?

There are several natural ways to test. One is the old Yankee pragmatism, does it work? Another is the European higher criticism of logic and reason, and tested in our day-to-day lives. A third is the scientific method of predictions and testing of the prediction of such a worldview. Against these stand long traditions that our world is in turmoil, there are no cause and effect relationships, reason and logic do not apply, and everything we do not understand is an act of God or the gods. In this latter case, our worldview is of a meaningless, random, capricious, unordered, unknowable nature. If we are going to compare our worldviews, it is important to understand these differences. It is even more important when considering more controversial subjects such as our beliefs in God. It provides little value to begin a discussion without first checking on our respective views.

The deepest aspect we can share in our lives is our worldview. It is the summary of all our experiences, knowledge, wisdom, beliefs and faiths. History has shown how slowly a cultural worldview changes. Or that these changes are necessarily in a positive direction. The Western countries have made great strides motivated by their worldview and due to the impact and success of the sciences. But many other aspects of our worldview have not changed or progressed. Our view of God is under attack. Thus, it is more important than ever to test our worldviews, including our faith.

NEW WORLD ORDER ················

I had it all figured out; I had developed a worldview and lifestyle that accommodated all I knew. It was a nice position and I was ready to enjoy this peace and stability in my retirement years. Yes, there had been the uneasy elements of a few minor wars and some terrorism now and then, but that all seemed reasonably under control and no major changes were necessary in my way of thinking and living. Then came along September 11, 2001 and the terrorist attacks on the US. There have been personal friends involved in many aspects of the resulting turmoil in our country. It is essential to re-think, re-plan and re-act to account for this New World Order.

My primary window into the world is the Hoover Institution at Stanford University, a research center with major archives and the mission statement, "Ideas Defining a Free Society." We have the opportunity to listen to editors of major newspapers and magazines; we have access to broad research topics from many academics around the US and from those working with President Bush, currently formulating policies. Since September 11, a major emphasis has been placed on terrorism. There have been many conferences, symposia, and seminars on this topic, from many different perspectives. Each of the speakers has provided background information and the problems we are facing with very little on the long-range solution. This is because of the complexity of the problem, the uncertainties, and the long time-period of achieving any significant changes.

As I sit back and sort through all this material, I come up with a lot of pieces, but little in the way of integrating the pieces and putting the summary into action. For example:

The terrorism problem is multi-faceted; it has caused upset in every aspect of our society. We have local problems, cultural problems, political problems, government problems, diplomatic problems, military problems, economical problems, energy problems, media (news, movies, entertainment & editorial) problems, medical problems, scientific problems, psychological problems, and even religions problems. In general, what one would call a God-sized problem.

In the presentations made at Standford, the implications were that major changes in the general way of life and thinking would be required to solve these problems. There are adaptations and techniques that can be used to bring our lives back to an almost normal existence, but there are transitions and developments needed to achieve this new state of normality. The terrorist problems really started back in the 1980s, and we are just now getting around to taking them seriously. It would seem it will take another twenty years, a generation, to get back to a stable condition. Can our nation stick together for twenty years of turmoil and change? How can we promote unity when undergoing change? Obviously one major factor is education, an other is leadership and a third is involvement. The education is a relatively simple process, the leadership is a challenge, and the involvement of everyone is an impossible dream (if you are not with us, you are against us).

Consider that if we are to make major changes, education and training are significant factors. If we are going to change, we need to know why, how and when to make these changes. There is a lot of planning and impact upon our time and finances. But it can be accomplished. Such changes are always necessary during a war. I can recall all the changes necessary during WW II. Leadership is also vital. Who is going to be the one or ones determining what needs to be done and how we are going to do it? We have many different factions, each with their own ideas and plans. In previous wars, the pattern was similar, except for the changes in technology. Now we have a major change in the techniques and tactics which affect how the war is waged. Careful planning is required.

The last element is getting everyone involved in the program. This requires a goal greater than our own self-interests, along with various incentives and enforcements. We are too quick to forgive and forget when, at the same time, there is no change in our opponents' determination to destroy our way of life. We look at everything as having a short time window, and this is not unusual or unexpected. Before, everything changed rapidly, and what was a problem today no longer existed the next day. However, there is no indication that terrorism will disappear so quickly, as the indoctrination of hate for the US is presently taught in schools and mosques in many Middle East countries. Terrorism has become a way of life for many. The New World Order.

REBUILDING OUR INTELLECTUAL FOUNDATION ················

Are we still operating with the intellectual foundation we set down in high school or college? Personally, there have been several changes since then, but not very often. It takes a major impact on my life to rebuild my intellectual foundation. Not always will I go back and rebuild it. Why should I? I have been using it successfully for many years; why change now? This question becomes more important as we transition into the retirement years. During the working years, our intellectual foundation is relatively stable, with perhaps a few minor changes as we change positions or even jobs. The basic system stays in place. There is little necessity to rebuild as long as things go along smoothly. In retirement, however, everything changes.

When the major changes come along, they interrupt our world perspective. Such major events include the death of a close friend or relative, having a major illness or operation with long recovery, changing from atheist or agnostic to a believer and follower of Jesus Christ, or significant changes in our scientific understanding of ourself and the world. The first two relate how fragile our life really is; there is only a small line that separates life from death. Life becomes more precious as we realize it is far from a permanent state. The third is a major change in our belief system—the acceptance of God's Truth. Not everyone changes their intellectual foundation; they may continue with two separate foundations, one for the weekday world of work, and another for Sunday and going to church. This is not a very stable condition; it would be better to expand and rebuild our intellectual foundation to include God and His Kingdom.

The last major change in our lives, that is, significant changes in science, relates to the knowledge and understanding of ourselves, our world and our universe. Consider, for instance, advances in genetics and chromosome research. These developments change the way we consider our health and life expectancy. There are whole new ways of relating people and people groups. It is a major breakthrough in understanding life. We have also made significant progress in understanding ecology and the relationship of cause and effects for what we do. We can make changes that improve the long-term living conditions on our planet.

Finally, the advances in astronomy and cosmology reveal first that the position of our earth is very special in its placement in our Milky Way Galaxy. We are in a very protected position. We are not near the center, where high radiation and gravity attractions would make life impossible; we are not in the dense centers of the spiral arms which have similar conditions. The more recent breakthrough has been in the dimensionality of our universe. We are living not in four dimensions—height, width, length and time—but in eleven dimensions, maybe more. At present we know very little about these other seven dimensions, other than that they are curled around the four we presently experience today.

The inputs from these major changes should cause us to rebuild our intellectual foundations. But it is in our retirement years that we do not want to change anything! To change when we are young is nothing new, there are always changes going on and, most of the time, we accept them naturally. During the working years, the changes come less often and are easy to accommodate. We naturally make changes when our family alters in number or age, we move from job to job or house to house, or acquire a special vacation place/activity. When it comes to older age and retirement, we slow down even more and changes become more difficult. What can we do to help the process?

The Scriptures provide a basic intellectual foundation that does not change because it is given by God, the Creator of all, who does not change. All else may change around us, but He does not, has not, and will not change. His Word is eternal. If we build our intellectual foundation on God's Word there will be no reason for change. I have found that my foundation significantly affects my interpretation and understanding of God's Word. Thus, I have a continuous process. It is not that God's Word has changed, but I have changed. I am continuously reinterpreting my intellectual foundation, but in smaller steps and in line with deeper understanding of Scripture. I find my limitations are in understanding Scripture. What at first may seem like a conflict or meaningless statement eventually will be perfectly logical and rational. It is all related to our experience and understanding of life that we find the value of God's Word.

....

CHAPTER 2

Philosophy of Life Examined

I like to sit back and think about the meaning of life, and, as I find little flashes of insight, to write these down and pass it along to others. Perhaps they will give a new perspective on looking at ourselves and our purpose for living. I believe that life is rational, meaningful and has purpose. These essays ponder the meaning of life, not just for my benefit, but to help us all in thinking about why we are here and what we are doing with our lives.

> The New Testament is uniformly consistent in seeing something as being wrong in man himself. These analyses of man are based on man's responsibility for his evil actions; they are not saying that it is simply his motions that have gone astray: it is man's will that is the central problem.
>
> Denis Alexander

CHILDREN PLAYING IN A SANDBOX ·············

When our grandchildren were younger, we had a large sandbox full of sand and all sorts of buckets, shovels, cars and trucks. The children had a ball, and played there for hours. It was fun to watch them playing. They were creative in what they would do and build. Their imaginations went wild in all sorts of directions. When they left, we had a big cover come down which kept the leaves, rain and local cats out of the sandbox. It was always ready when they would come next time. They have now grown beyond the sandbox age, but I still remember back to those days.

As I think of all the activities and projects I have worked on these many years, I get the image that, as adults, we are still playing in a giant sandbox. God made our world to be like an adult sandbox. Almost everything we could want is provided for in His sandbox. We can build large homes, cities and nations, but eventually it will all turn back into a sandbox. We do not bring anything into the sandbox and we do not take anything out when we leave. Conditions are reasonably the same from generation to generation. Just our toys get a little more complex. Can this really be a true perspective on life? Are we just children playing in God's sandbox?

One of my special joys in life is studying astronomy and cosmology. These two fields have made incredible advances in the past ten years. The sensitivity of present telescopes and special instruments has extended our view out almost to the beginning of time. The discoveries show a universe of enormous size, magnitude and complexity, numbers that go far beyond anything we encounter in earth's sandbox. Our largest thermo-nuclear bombs are like tossing up a spoon of sand compared to the magnitude of the exploding stars and the radiations from black holes. The size alone of the galaxies shrinks our world to just the size of a small sandbox. If it were not for the fact that we are near the edge of the Milky Way Galaxy and in between two of the major spiral arms, our environment would be far too hostile for life. Our world is a very protected sandbox.

Some insist our world is one of chance among many possibilities, while others strongly believe it is designed by a loving God. The sandbox I built for our grandchildren was one of careful design, provided with all the toys and protected from the sun, rain, animals and trees around us. It was a safe place to play. One could insist that the sandbox in our backyard just happened by chance, but it just does not seem logical. The more we study and learn about our world, the more special and unique it becomes.

I can imagine God looking down on all His children playing in His sandbox, our world, and having great joy. But what is even more special is for His children to recognize that He built it for them. He wants to interact with His children just as we enjoyed interacting with our grandchildren and sharing their adventures in the sandbox. It is far too easy to get so involved in the day to day activities in our sandbox, that we lose contact with God and all His provisions. We miss the larger picture of what life in the sandbox is all about. The great adventure of the sandbox is to realize and accept that it was all created by God. It is through life in the sandbox that we find God. How can this be?

The simple reality is that life in the sandbox is meaningless, purposeless, and relationshipless without recognizing that it is God's creation of love, and that He has a higher meaning, purpose and relationship for His children, not in a temporal passing world, but in an eternal world He has prepared for us when we leave our earthly sandbox. God sent His Son, Jesus, down to our sandbox to show us how to play. It is as we follow Him and let Him be Lord of our life, that we come into full relationship with God as His children. All others will be cast aside because they have not grown in love for God our Father.

WHO DO YOU THINK YOU ARE? • • • • • • • • • • • • • •

We spend much of our lives trying to figure out who we are. We get information from many different places. Our parents give us their version of who we are and where we are going. So do our many friends and the teachers who interact with us at school. If we go to church, there are the Sunday school classes and the preacher's sermons. When we go to work, our boss and fellow employees also give definition of who we are. If we get married, our mates have something to say about this also. All are about telling us who we are. But how do they know? Who told them? And how do we know they are correct?

Now, if they all gave the same message, we might have a chance of figuring this all out. But if you have had similar experiences like mine, the messages are very, very mixed; they seldom agree. For example, doctors early in my life, when I was around five years old or so, warned me about any physical activity during which I could have gotten bumped or fallen down, as they considered my eyes physically weak and I, therefore, could easily go blind. I have not gone blind yet, but without glasses my vision is defined as legally blind. Many times in grade school the teachers implied I was hopeless; I have quite a collection of "F's" to prove that. But there were a few who gave me hope. Then in high school, the counselor said, "Don't plan on college, you will never make it. Learn a trade and go that way!" Shortly after that I got accepted to Stanford University as a physics major. When I was in graduate school, I talked to the pastor about joining his church. He basically said, "We are not interested in you becoming a member," implying that I was not good enough.

That was Menlo Park Presbyterian Church where I am now a member. Things do change.

When I began the search of who I was, my idea was that I could be anybody I wanted to be. None of the suggestions I had received earlier made any sense. So I looked around and picked one. I wanted to be like Albert Einstein. I loved the sciences and mathematics, and most other subjects were a total loss. Just think, daydreaming about the Grand Universal Theory of the Universe! If Einstein did the E = mc^2 thing, and the General Theory of Relativity, then I should be able to do the next best thing. So off in this direction I began to climb. University physics classes were easy but math was a little challenging—it was so abstract and difficult to create images. On to theoretical physics classes—these also were getting more difficult as there was not a natural bridge to experience and logic. Quantum mechanics was just out there as more math logic than physics, as it seemed to me. I far more enjoyed doing the hands-on stuff, and was not all that excited about getting a better solution to an integral-differential equation or developing a grand tensor matrix solution to a theoretical problem. My dream was beginning to crumble.

In graduate school I switched to electrical engineering, the more hands-on stuff, but still on the theoretical and research side. At that time EE also included communications, electro-magnetic propagation, computers, information theory and statistics, so that was still going in a good direction. Today, I am still going in this direction. These are still my great interests, activities and goals in retirement. The fulfillment comes now in astronomy, getting out the telescope and taking pictures of all those marvelous deep space images and studying the physics involved. Even more hands-on is designing, building, running and maintaining a railroad in the back yard, one big enough that people can ride on. That is all more than enough to keep me busy and focused on who I am.

I am still working on the Grand Universal Theory of the Universe. But now I have some good help and a teacher. God came along and said, "I created it all. If you want to find out all about this, come and ask me!" I have been very busy talking to God about this universe He created. He gives me a lot of homework to do. He has produced a question and answer book for beginner, and I am still working on that—the Bible. However, there is far, far more to His creation than is in that book. Not only am I learning about the universe, I am also learning about myself and what He created me to be. Life is a lot easier when you have a good guide, but at the rate we are going, it is going to take a number of centuries to get it all figured out. Besides, God seems far more interested in our relationship and having fun than getting all my problems solved in a hurry. It is through God that I am finally finding out who I am. After all, God created me. All the others were just guessing.

WAITING FOR THE SUNRISE ················

Each day at our beach-front condo in Kauai, I go out to watch the sunrise. The day cannot begin without observing the dramatic changes from night to day. Many are similar, but no two are identical, as the clouds vary along the horizon. There is the first sign of light overcoming the black of night. Then very gradually the East becomes a brighter and brighter light blue. The clouds begin to take on a dull purple-red glow, slowly brightening into the oranges, the yellows and the gold. Last of all, the great glowing ball of the sun comes slowly into view, distorted into an egg shape from the atmospheric refraction. I constantly look for the green flash, but have only seen it once—it does take especially clear viewing conditions. From this point shadows are cast across the land and day has begun. It is a long, majestic process. What a regal way to start the day!

The sunrise is but a mechanical process all caused by the rotation of the earth. We are not seeing the sunrise at all, only the natural, monotonous, repeated cycle of the transition between night and day. No big deal, it happens the same every day and can be calculated as accurately as we could possible want. Why even bother to get up or, if one is up, why bother to look? Often the clouds hide the process and you really never get to see the sunrise at the horizon anyway. It has been the same for billions of years in the past and will be the same for billions of years into the future. We should spend our time on something more important!

Once the sun is up, the business of the day can begin. Our routine falls into place and life is as though night never occurred. All the past concerns and nightmares of the dark have passed and there is joy in the daylight. What could not be seen in the darkness, is now clearly visible in the daylight. What were vague outlines, are now seen in full detail. What a difference the sun makes in the world around us and how it impacts our lives. The sun brings joy, peace and meaning to life.

Sun up? What's the big deal? We can generate sufficient light ourselves that we do not need the sun. Who cares if the sun is up or down? We can go on just as well without it! In fact, maybe even better. Just think, no sun to blind you when driving in the morning or evenings. During the day we would not have to worry about wearing hats, dark glasses or putting on sun-block; we could just go out without worry. Also, without the sun, the temperature would be constant—we could wear the same clothes all day, all month and all year long. We would not need a big wardrobe. And no problems with traveling—it would be the same temperature and conditions everywhere. What a deal!

There is another sunrise I am waiting for. This is the second return of Jesus Christ, God's Son. For some, this is the long-awaited event of all history. A time when the trumpets of Heaven will sound and Christ will return in great power and glory; more spectacular than any sunrise. Oh what a wonderful day that will be. Christ will rule as King of kings and Lord of lords. All things will be made right and holy. For those who believe in Jesus Christ and have accepted Him as Lord of their life, our Saviour will come. What a grand and glorious day that will be. All darkness will be banished and light of God will prevail in truth, peace and joy.

God coming to earth again? Just a big joke—a myth believed by those too weak to do anything on their own. It has not happened in the past and therefore it will not happen in the future. The sciences have not found God, so therefore He does not exist. Forget about it; it is just a big waste of time and gets people unnecessarily stirred up. Takes their minds off the real, productive work. We have all we need, it just requires getting people organized and motivated. The big, new, world government will solve all those petty conflicts around the world. We can do anything if we just put our minds to it. Out of our way; we're moving forward.

We have two opposite realities to choose. One, a world of science and political power welded together to control the world and all its inhabitants. To be run like one large machine. Our only hope to survive by our own power, might and intelligence. The other, the overwhelming creative power of God who loves us and will save us from the destruction and death which is coming to our earth. Our salvation depends upon our love and acceptance of Jesus Christ as our Lord. It is by faith we are saved and not by works. Choose today which way to go; your future depends upon it.

WE WANT THE RIGHT ANSWER! ··············

There was an old story about a General who had a serious problem. He ordered the Colonel to assemble a committee to provide a solution to his problem. The committee presented their results, but the General rejected them: "This is not the right answer, find another committee." And again, another committee studied the problem and submitted their findings. Again the General said, "This is not the right answer, find another committee." After eight committees, the General finally got the right answer! This may be a little extreme, but we all have a sense of what the right answer should be. And we want the right answer! We continue to search in order to find the right answer.

But what if the right answer is not the answer we want to hear? We have a problem. Is it possible for us to accept an answer that is not our right answer? In many cases, we will not accept an answer that is outside our acceptance zone. How can this be? What are the driving conditions that determine our "recognition" of the right answer?

I have a very strong opinion about what the right answer should be. After all, I have been around for some sixty-plus years and have learned a thing or two. If the answer I get is not what I expect, I persistently keep looking. It takes me a very long time and a lot of pressure to make a decision to accept something other than my right answer. There is a long chain of subconscious logic embedded in the acceptance process. First, I generally have an opinion on the answer and range of possibilities I expect. Second, it must be consistent with all the other information I have on the particular subject. Third, I evaluate the reliability and authority of the source of the answer. Fourth,

I carefully review the impact of accepting an answer different than my pre-approved answer. Fifth, I wait a long, long time before making any difficult decisions, like accepting an answer other than the one I want. Waiting increases the possibility of other answers coming up. Sixth, I ask the Lord in prayer for guidance and wisdom in making decisions. This is followed by seven: asking all my friends and associates who may be able to provide helpful information, for their advice. Nevertheless, for any answer other than the right one, acceptance is a very slow process and is always subject to reversal.

So why am I surprised at Dr. Gerald Schroeder's *Genesis and the Big Bang,* where the end of the book has a section which derides religious leaders for not accepting proven scientific facts and using them in their theology, and which equally chastises scientific leaders for postulating ridiculous theories just to deny creation and the possible existence of God. Both sides refuse to accept an answer that is not the expected and approved right answer. This does not mean that everyone on both sides of the issue are actively fighting each other, but that the majority opinion, the accepted right answer, is totally different on both sides. Perhaps my problem is that I expect everyone to agree and accept a carefully prepared and presented proof for resolving any question. In retrospect, I must admit that I am probably as biased as any of them, just in other areas, and don't see it. Subconsciously, I still want my right answer!

God must get frustrated at times when we refuse to accept the truth and wisdom He presents to us in a clear and concise way. Here we are, enjoying His creation but refusing to accept both Him and His creation and all that has been revealed to us. We want to choose what revelations we accept—the right answers of course. After all, we would not want to accept a false or partially correct answer. If we really are honest, aren't all our answers both partial truths and partial falsehoods? How can we possibly know the whole right answer, since the real answer has both a physical and a spiritual aspect?

I have occasionally taken tests where there are no wrong answers, typically multiple choice. A parallel aspect is when it is announced, "There are no dumb questions." I believe God loves us so much that He tells us there are no wrong answers and there are no dumb questions, so long as they are within the spectrum of good; it is all part of the free will He has given us. We are, though, responsible and held accountable for our dumb questions and wrong answers, outside of that spectrum. If we seek to ask the right questions and search for the right answers, God will reward us. The big question is, do we believe God and have faith in the answers He gives us? If so, we will accept His offer of forgiveness and salvation by following the answers given to us by His Son, Jesus Christ. He has all the right answers!

THE FAMILY CONNECTION ················

There are many different "connections" between people. We first think of the family connection or unit. There is a closeness of concern and protection in the strong family, which is as it should be. We are not independent survivors at birth, nor are we in all phases of life, especially as the latter years approach.

For many, there is a neighborhood connection, particularly if they have lived in the same place for a long time and know those living around them. There is a common concern and protection for the neighborhood.

Then we come to work; there is a natural teamwork that takes place. We are all dependent on each other to get all the work done. And so it goes upward to our city, county, state, nation, hemisphere and the world. One way or another, we are all part of a larger family; there are family connections.

For some there is a natural rebellion against these connections, the ties that bind us; they feel dominated and controlled by them and are trying to find themselves. Is our only value and significance through our family connection? Don't we have a worth and importance all by ourselves? Perhaps so, but all the evaluations of who we are come from all our connections with people around us. In what other way can we be evaluated? Do we have any other technique of evaluation other then comparing people, classifying people, analyzing people, measuring people and observing people? Is it only through our connections with people that we can be evaluated. This can be very dangerous; isn't there some other way to establish ourselves? If not, we are subject to the popularity pole or the achievement rewards! But there is another way!

There is a source outside ourselves, our world and our universe. This source is God. He freely communicates His evaluation of us through His Word, the Bible, and through the Holy Spirit, one of the Trinity. God created us in His image and has great love for us. God looked at all He created and said, "It is good, very good." He is eager for us to rejoin His family and become His children. We are born alienated from God, as children of this world, due to the temptations of Satan and the great Fall of Adam and Eve. From this point on, the human race has been deceived and mislead through the works of Satan. There is, however, a way back to the family of God. It is through His Son, Jesus Christ, who came to earth, suffered death for our transgressions, and was resurrected in life and brought back to Heaven as King of kings and Lord of lords and our Saviour. In repenting of our rebellion and accepting Jesus as our Lord, we are reunited into God's family. Being part of God's family has great value and honor. However, there is more to it than this.

Consider what the Bible says about God's family members in Acts 9. Saul was breathing murderous threats against the Lord's disciple and followers and was on his way to Damascus searching for any who were followers of Jesus. Verses 3 and 4 reveal this:

> *As he neared Damascus on his journey, suddenly a light from heaven flashed around him. He fell to the ground and heard a voice saying to him, "Saul, Saul, why do you persecute me?" "Who are you, Lord?" Saul asked. "I am Jesus, whom you are persecuting," he replied....*

Can we imagine that, as Christians on earth are being persecuted, this is also persecuting our Lord Jesus? Isn't this just like any close family? If any member of the family is mistreated or harmed, this effects the entire family. It is as though the act was administered to the whole family! Each member who hears about the tragedy is affected. Jesus is closely connected to His family of believers. What they feel and suffer, He also feels and suffers. God can act quickly, decisively and powerfully to protect us, but it is His option and in His overall plan that everything must take place.

We remember Daniel in the lions' den where an angel protected him (Daniel 6:16–23). Then Shadrach, Meshach and Abend-nego, who were put in the fiery furnace and were not burned (Daniel 3:19–26). God has promised to be with us, to guide us and protect us in Satan's world. Consider the Psalm 23, verse 4,

> *Even though I walk through the valley of the shadow of death, I will fear no evil for you are with me; your rod and your staff, they comfort me.*

God our Father can deliver us from all evil. As Children of God, our heavenly family connection provides all we need and is a present reminder each time we worship together. It is with our mutual concern and support for our struggles on earth as we follow our Lord Jesus that we build our family connection.

YOU DON'T CHANGE PEOPLE, YOU CHANGE PEOPLE'S KIDS ··············

Have you ever tried to change someone? This includes what they do, what they say, how they react and many other of the social graces or work ethics. It is very hard to change people. Consider our jails. Almost all inmates are repeat offenders. One would think that if we are going to change someone, the jail is about as serious as we can get without just eliminating them. Or, consider the divorce rate, which is over fifty percent. The couples all started out with good intentions and perhaps some ideas that the other partner would change a little. However, it does not work that easily. My experience of changing people comes from a management position. The employees were motivated by promotions, salary increases, choices of jobs and other subtle conditions of work. Some people just fit in to the work system and others did not. In trying to change those who did not naturally go along with the plan, it was easier to transfer them or lay them off than to achieve any change. Why is this?

When we come to children, it is a very different story. Children are generally open to new ideas and new ways of doing things. They are generally trying to please the adults in their lives. In addition, everything around them, including themselves, is changing. Their growth patterns represent continual changes. They have not fixed their personality, their interests and their likes and dislikes. These things go though several changes and refinements. Slowly and surely these patterns get fixed, which shape them into adults, and they become unchangeable, for the most part. This puts a major responsibility on parents, teachers, family, and society. Does

125

this leave the adults a hopeless case for change? Isn't there something we can do?

Let us consider what it takes for an adult to change. First there must be mental assertion for the need for change. This is a brain process including reason, logic, intuition, feelings, emotions and a developed plan of how to change. It is not coincidence that the first plan a person develops is usually impractical and will not work. It generally requires help and insight from those around them and the support for the change. In adults, change is not the natural process that is readily accepted as in childhood. Second, the body needs to be in alignment and compatible for this change. It is not obvious that the conscious brain is in total control of the body. There are a great number of automatic control systems not under conscious manipulations, for example, the heart rate, food digestion, hormone production, and responses of our senses. There are those systems under partial control, such as breathing, scratching an itch, what our mind is thinking, and the direction in which we look. Along with these, we mostly control the movement of our arms, legs, body and what we talk about. The point of all this is that we are not totally in control of ourselves. To make major changes requires all body functions to change in one way or another. In many cases we cannot make those changes by ourselves. Thus the old saying, "You don't change people…"

Is change thus hopeless? Should we just give up and accept who and what we are? No way! Change is possible, but it most likely will take someone greater than ourselves to help us. I am reminded of Paul's comments in Romans 7:15,19,24–25:

I do not understand what I do. For what I want to do I do not do, but what I hate I do… For what I do is not the good I want to do; no, the evil I do not want to do— this I keep on doing. Now if I do what I do not want to do, it is no long I who do it, but it is sin living in me that does it… What a wretched man I am! Who will rescue me from this body of death? Thanks be to God— through Jesus Christ our Lord!

God is able to change us, to rescue us from the entrapment of ourselves. God is in the business of changing people and He is very good at it. But we must accept Him as our Lord, and want to change our ways, before He will come in and guild and empower the changes in our lives. They may not be exactly the changes we want, but they are the changes we need. He will even help us understand and accept the changes and plans He has for our lives. As for our kids, the sooner they find and accept Jesus as their Lord and Savior, the better. It is much easier to accept the Lord when we are young and open to change, than as adults fixed in our ways.

JUSTICE AND MERCY ••••••••••••••

How can we have both justice and mercy? It would seem to me that justice has no room for mercy and mercy has no room for justice. Now why should that be? Our symbol of justice is a blindfolded judge holding scales. The judge is only to weigh the facts—"The truth, the whole truth, and nothing but the truth, so help us God." This does not include a correction factor for mercy; just follow the law. Mercy, on the other hand, considers we are all humans and therefore subject to making mistakes, having poor judgement and having strong emotions at times. Thus, we should not be held accountable for our fallible humanness. There have been some attempts at combining justice and mercy by passing laws that have a range of punishments which the judge can use in a show of the court's mercy. Also, in jury trials, the jury in its deliberations may come to a verdict more on the basis of mercy than on the carrying-out of justice. They consider many other factors involved in the case that are more subjective than objective. Often justice depends upon the conservative or liberal disposition of the judge and jury and, of course, the ability of the defending and prosecuting lawyers in presenting their cases. A very good defense lawyer makes a big difference in the outcome of justice.

Is this the best we can do—some justice and some mercy? Why can't we have full justice and full mercy? After all, that is what we would like. We read about cases where the justice of the law is carried out in full measure and the person is eventually shown to be innocent. In other cases, such as with the "Three Strikes and You Are Out" law, a minor criminal will end up in jail for life with no chance of release. On the other side, there are those whom everyone believes are guilty, but there is not sufficient evidence to convict them. In our court system, one is innocent until proven guilty, beyond any reasonable doubt. Therefore, many guilty are given mercy when they do not deserve it. There are also cases where the police or others involved mishandle the evidence and the case is dismissed. The more justice is pursued, the less mercy, and the more innocents are sent to jail. The less justice is vigorously pursued, the more mercy is shown, and the more guilty are released into society. We may even question the whole system of justice where about eighty percent of the crimes are committed by single males from sixteen to twenty-four years of age and generally unemployed. And, the probably of a person sent to jail repeating a criminal act once released is also around eighty percent. By all measures, our justice system is not very effective.

Back in the 1760s, in Colonial Williamsburg, justice was much simpler. Because there was no efficient system of records or identifying people, the perpetrators' crimes were often branded onto their forehead for all to see. For simple crimes, the person was put in blocks in the town square. For serious crimes, there was a jail sentence, but since the people considered more than two weeks to be cruel and unusual punishment, a person was executed for the very serious crimes—this was considered a show of mercy. From accounts of the time, this justice system was quite effective.

There is another system of justice we must consider, that is, God's system of justice and mercy. God has perfect information on everything a person has done and thought, so there is no question about the evidence. Next, His law of justice is very simple, "Break one or more laws and the penalty is death." He also knows that the probability of us breaking one or more of His laws is absolute. We begin as sinners and only get worse. God's justice thus finds us all guilty and subject to death. So where is the mercy? God's Son, Jesus Christ, has stepped up and said He will take our place; He will die for us. It is Jesus who shows us divine mercy so that justice may be carried out. There is, however, one condition in Jesus' mercy. We must repent of our many sins and promise to follow and obey Him to the best of our abilities. In comparison to our human justice systems, God's plan is far more effective and shows great compassion and mercy. However, the penalty for those who do not accept Jesus' offer of mercy is far worse than anything our world has to offer. Choose this day to accept Jesus' offer of mercy and be assured of an eternal life of joy.

THE RULE OF LAW ················

We are a nation of laws—hundreds, thousands, millions and probably billions of them. There are laws dictating where I can put lights in our yard. There are laws specifying where light switches can be put in our house. And even my wife has laws about when the lights can be turned on and when they must be turned off. All our social, religious, work, play and government groups have laws on how things are to be done. If I drive a car, there are laws. If I make money there are laws on how much the IRS and every other government agency can take in taxes and fees. There is no way I can know all these laws, much less understand or follow them. Besides, people are constantly changing and adding to all these laws. Nevertheless, ignorance of the law is no excuse!

I have to believe that life was much simpler in Jesus' time on earth. Yes, the Jews had laws. In fact, they kept inventing new laws to explain the old laws. Fortunately they were limited by not having computers, lots of paper or printing presses. Moses had passed down only ten laws from God. Now that seems very simple and easy compared to our present times, but the Jews had trouble following those ten laws. As a result, the Scribes and Pharisees began to simplify and explain these laws so they could be understood and followed easily. They ended up with many more laws. There were great debates among the lawyers of that day about which were the important laws and which were the lesser laws. One lawyer went to Jesus and asked him,

"Teacher, which is the greatest commandment in the Law?" Jesus replied, "Love the Lord your God with all

131

your heart and with all your soul and with all your mind. This is the first and greatest commandment. And the second is like it: Love your neighbor as yourself. All the Laws and the Prophets hang on these two commandments" (Matthew 22:36–40).

Now that is great!

There are three aspects to The Rule of Law. One is the law itself, the second is how the law is enforced, and the third is the penalty for breaking the law. Consider first the physical laws of our universe. We cannot break these laws, we are part of them; they are built into our nature. To go "against" these laws requires energy, force and intelligence. It would be more correct to say we are using the laws of nature for our benefit, rather than implying that we are breaking them.

Next, consider the civil laws of our nation. They are created by governments for our protection and to bring order in the land. They establish relationships between property, people and principalities. They are enforced by various policing agencies, and penalties are prescribed by the law, with the more serious cases reviewed by the courts. The penalties can be financial or include incarceration. The limitations of these laws is that those who violate them must be caught and have sufficient evidence for conviction. Even then, it is up to the courts and the lawyers' arguments on both sides, to determine guilt. It is far from a perfect system.

The last set of laws are the ethical, moral and religious laws. God has basically said, "Break one of My Laws and you are dead!" Well, it isn't quite all that sudden and abrupt, as enforcement may not occur until you physically die. God is considering your eternal spiritual life, whether we end up in

Heaven or Hell. However, there are also real and natural impacts on our physical life from breaking God's Laws.

Laws do not produce order, ethics, morality, justice, compassion, mercy, love or peace. Why do we have laws? Is it because God gave us Ten Laws with a penalty of death, and we still don't know how to follow them? We develop more laws and less penalties! Is it because our universe is governed by physical laws based on time, force and energy? We work very hard on inventing ways to use energy, force and time to get round the natural laws! Perhaps it is our nature; we are in total rebellion against any authority, laws or restrictions. We go around deaf, dumb and blinded to the basis for all these laws. Laws are made to help us guide our lives as we walk on earth.

Consider Paul's comments in Romans 7:22–25,

For in my inner being I delight in God's law, but I see another law at work in the members of my body, waging war against the law of my mind and making me a prisoner of the law of sin at work within my members. ...Who will rescue me from this body of death? Thanks be to God—through Jesus Christ our Lord!

It is only by following our Lord Jesus that He gives us the strength, guidance and understanding through the indwelling Holy Spirit to follow God's laws. The degree to which we can follow Christ is the degree to which we can follow God's Laws. God's Law and the corresponding human laws give us guides to show how well we are doing in following the Rule of Law.

My record is not very good.

THE SIZE OF OUR PROBLEMS ··············

I rank my problems by size; there are big ones, medium size ones and small ones. Now, there are problems that do not fit in my sizing scales. For example, death. This problem is too big to fit into my perspective. And there are problems that are too small to fit, such as when I lose one hair. I have too many of them to count. This hair loss will eventually get large enough to surface as a hair problem, but not a single hair issue. The basic philosophy is that I only rank problems I can do something about. If I cannot do something about it, it is not a problem I can handle, so it is dropped. However, I do include problems I may not be able to solve or change directly, but that someone else can. These include going to the doctor, writing letters to government agencies and politicians, or going to my friends and neighbors. This is the way I organize my problems.

There is another category of problems—the problems I cannot do anything about, but I still worry about them. However, I can do something about the worry even if I do not attack the basic problem. An example of this are all the changes that come with aging. I can do very little about them but I can classify the size of my worry problems; these go in my problems-to-be-solved list as small, medium or large. There are many approaches to resolving the worrying over problems that can not be changed. Thus my problems are still organized.

A third category of problems are those we have, but we do not know we have or are not willing to recognize we have; at least for now. In this category I include heart disease, cancer, addictions, psychological disorders, genetic problems and such. These are problems we have not yet included in our problem matrix. Thus, for all practical purposes, these problems do not exist; at least for us.

There is even a fourth category of problems. These are serious problems that are too big for us, our friends, our doctors or our government to handle. We must do something about them, but we can't. These I classify as the God-Sized Problems. Examples here are major natural disasters, such as fire, storms, draught, earthquakes or plagues. I would even include some local and world wars in this category. Although wars are begun by governments, they quickly get out of control because of governments. These problems are beyond the resources we can muster. However, there are still some who believe that all we need is a larger government and then we would not need God. That is, a large world government could handle all these problems and there would be nothing left for God to do! This is not my perspective.

What we have yet to do is to check God's perspective on our problems. Consider the Scriptures. Matthew 10:30, *"And even the very hairs of your head are all numbered."* brings us down to the small details. For a bigger perspective, see Psalm 147:4, *"He determines the number of the stars and calls them each by name."* When we consider the present estimate of a thousand billion billion stars, that is a very large number of very big objects. And God pays attention to us all the way down to the number of hairs on our head? Incredible! What can we conclude?

We do not understand "small" from a large perspective. Compared to our Solar System, we are tiny, tiny. Compared to our Milky Way galaxy, we are infinitesimal. Compared to the universe with billions upon billions of galaxies, we are totally insignificant! On the other hand, we do not understand "small" from a small perspective. Compared to a virus or bacteria we are very large. Compared to an atom, we are huge. And compared to sub-nuclear particles, we are so large as to approach infinity. The size of our largest problems never reaches universal proportions and our miniscule problems are tremendously gigantic compared to the sub-nuclear particles. It is all a matter of perspective. And, God works all the details. There is nothing too small or too large for God. He is in control of it all; to be in control includes knowing, seeing and caring for all.

TRANSFORMING OUR "?" INTO "!" ··············

If you are like me, there are a lot of unanswered questions in life. How can we straighten out our questions marks into exciting explanation points? Where can we turn for the answers? To our universities? I have done that and came out with more "?"s than "!"s. Perhaps, then, the professional world with all its experts and knowledge. Been there and still more "?"s than "!"s. There must be some great reservoir of answers to go with all our questions. But where should we look?

The best source for guidance on changing "?" into "!" is the Bible. It is not that every answer is given in the words of the Bible, but that the Bible gives us the *source* of all the answers to our questions. And not just any old answer, but answers that come alive and give inspiration. This translates into the transformation of doubts and concerns to joy and celebration. We are to turn to God with all our questions—the big ones and the very little ones. As we love and trust God, He will lead us to all the answers that satisfy our deepest longings. Who else could answer all our questions but He who created us and the universe we live in? He who loves us with a never-ending love.

Is it possible for us to come up with a question God cannot answer? What does that imply, that we know something that God does not know? For example, has God lived as a human, and did He know all the pain, suffering and grief we go through? Yes, Jesus, God's Son, did come to earth, live among people and die a horrible death. But that was only one time and one place. What about all of us; each one of us? God could not answer each of our questions

137

unless He was directly and intimately connected with us! He would have to know our very deepest thoughts, feelings and emotions, otherwise He is no better than our family, friends and counselors. For God to be able to answer all our questions requires Him to not only know every smallest detail about our lives and our future, but also about everyone and everything around us! How BIG is our God?

God can only answer our questions as long as we allow Him to be bigger then our questions. The bigger our questions, the bigger must be our vision of God. It is not that we determine God's true size, but that we will not accept answers from God that are bigger then our image of God. That is to say, we control our relationship with God. The bigger our God, the greater our relationship with Him. To get all our answers from God, we must accept an infinite God. Yes, God is infinite!

Furthermore, to change "?" into "!" requires that we receive not just ordinary answers, but answers that encourage, inspire and excite us! Not just "book" answers of facts, but answers with love. An answer that leads us forward. An answer that brings enlightenment and satisfaction and completeness. It is not just any answer we seek from God, but the truth that leads to abundant life.

This is not to say that I have liked all of God's answers to my questions. I most often want a short, immediate and fix-it answer, whereas God is interested in growth, maturity and sanctification. His answers most often include change—not doing it my way, but His way. When I can finally get around to agreeing with Him, all works out much better than my plans ever would have. That is when my "?" turn into "!" and I give Him all the praise and glory.

Next time, try asking God about your questions and do it His way for a change. See if the results are not changing your "?" into "!"

SEARCHING FOR FOOD, WATER AND SHELTER

The common essentials for life are considered to be food, water and shelter. If we have these basic physical needs we should be satisfied. However that is not what I observe in human nature. If we have food, we want a lot of it and not necessarily what is best for us. Given a chance, we would start with desserts. More than half of our population is overweight; people eat too much and of the wrong types of foods. We need water to keep the body functioning, but we generally want to do something with the water, so we drink coffee, soda pop, fruit drinks, beer and other substances. These are generally not as good for us as drinking straight water, but we like them better. (An interesting trend is drinking bottled water, which is really very expensive, more so than such things as gasoline for our cars.)

Now we come to shelters; everyone needs a roof over their heads. I find if we have a 500 square foot shelter, we want a 1,000 square foot one. And if we have a 1,000 square foot one, we want a 2,000 square foot one. On and on goes the size of what is considered necessary for our shelter. It seems the bigger they are, the more we must put in them. Some have all the facilities of a small city built into their home, i.e., a bar, workshop, exercise gym, concert hall, library, movie theater, restaurant (large kitchen and dinner room), school (study), hotel (extra bed & bath rooms), art gallery, furniture show room, clothing display closets, garage, and finally a junk storage facility. These houses get so big that extra staff are needed to run and maintain them. When are we ever satisfied with our food, water and shelter?

140

There must be something missing in our search for these basic physical needs. After all, we do not observe the animals eating more than they need, or requiring special drinking water. And as for shelter, the minimum serviceable area is adequate. A few may overdo it such as the gophers in my yard, but that is described as just going after their food. Thus, why are we so much different than the animals? Is there something missing in our search for the basic physical needs?

The answer is obviously, yes, there is something missing. However there is far from universal agreement on what the missing elements are. From the Scriptures we note that we are more than physical beings, we are also spiritual beings. We also need our spiritual food, water and shelter. Perhaps we are trying to pacify our spiritual needs with our physical acquisitions. Then we wonder why we are never satisfied. Consider Galations 5:22–23, regarding the fruits of spiritual satisfaction: *"love, joy, peace, patience, kindness, goodness, faithfulness, gentleness and self-control."* As long as we have needs, our missing elements, we cannot show forth this degree of acceptance. We cannot suppress our drive for survival which requires both physical and spiritual nourishment. And, without satisfying our internal needs, we are in no position to reach out to others in love, joy, peace and all the other fruits of the spirit.

The Scriptures also address our need for spiritual food, water and shelter. Consider John 4:32 where Jesus says, *"I have food to eat that you know nothing about."* Then in Exodus 16:35, *"The Israelites ate manna forty years."* This manna was most likely a combination of physical and spiritual food that came from Heaven. We also have the Word of God as our spiritual food to feed our soul. There is John 4:14 where Jesus said, *"Indeed, the water I give him will become in him a spring of water welling up to eternal life."* This is a reference to spiritual water. See also, Revelation 22:1, *"Then the angel showed me the river of the water of life, as clear as crystal, flowing from the throne of God and the Lamb...."* Regarding shelter we have Psalm 91:1, *"He who dwells in the shelter of the Most high will rest in the shadow of the Almighty."* Or perhaps Isaiah 32:1–2, *"See, a king will reign in righteousness and rulers will rule with justice. Each man will be like a shelter...."* To summarize, we have in Matthew 6:31–33:

> *So do not worry, saying, "What shall we eat?" or "What shall we drink?" or "What shall we wear?" For the pagans run after all these things, and your heavenly Father knows that you need them. But seek first his kingdom and his righteousness, and all these things will be given to you as well.*

Our spiritual needs are greater than our physical needs, not only in this life, but even more so for eternity.

THE PARADOX, ATTACHED BUT DETACHED ••••

There is a dilemma, a conundrum, an enigma, a mystery. The world around us, including ourselves, is both attached and detached at the same time. We are both united and separated. We are joined together and independent. How can this be?

Let us consider a simple example of time and space. We are joined together in time but severed in space. We must share the same time but it is totally impossible to share the same space. This, of course, applies to the living and not the dead or unborn. In the latter two cases the same space can be shared but not the same time. Why might this be?

Perhaps this is the physical nature of dimensionality. We cannot exist in all the same dimensions at once; one of them must be different. If all dimensions are exactly the same, then whatever occupies them must also be identical and not separable—sort of a mathematical theorem or a law of physics.

From a philosophical viewpoint, it would be impossible to distinguish between objects if they occupied the same time and space. To identify them would require separating them. To identify requires differences, some distinguishing features somewhere. The wonder of the universe, our world and ourselves, is our uniqueness. However, to have this uniqueness, we must also share the same existence.

Now that we are totally confused, let us examine some of the more common elements of being attached and detached. Consider the United States of America; each state is an independent unit but combines to make a nation of states, preserving the uniqueness and needs of the individual states, but combining resources for the common good and protection of the nation. And so goes the geopolitical structure throughout the world. The concept of a One-World Order and Ecumenical Movement of Churches where all are joined together in a common system is counter to all natural structures and requirements. Even all major corporations separate themselves into divisions for efficiency and effectiveness; each division has a unique mission statement.

The sciences are subdivided into specialities with words and expressions unique to each field. This is essential when focusing on the more detailed processes, experiments, and analyses. There is some combining of sciences, but this takes place in engineering specialities and not as part of the basic sciences. Engineering, when combined with manufacturing, finance and distribution, creates the vast array of technologies we have available in our society. There is a synergistic relationship where the total is greater than the sum of the individual pieces.

When we get down to culture and traditions we find even more examples. One of the big examples of today is the separation of Church and State. The failure of the present movement in the West is to totally detach the two without recognizing that the State has a serious need for the support of the Church. This need characterizes instability in the State. On the other hand, in the Middle East, the Church is becoming totally integrated with the State, which, in a different way, also leads to instability in the State. There is a very fine line of attachment and detachment between Church and State for them both to exist in a symbiotic relationship.

Taking one step further, consider our relationship with God—are we united or separated? What might this mean? If we were totally united with God, we would surrender all our free will and identity; basically we would be robots. If we were totally separated from God, we would live out our own self-interests and have no part in His love, salvation and eternity with Him. What we seem to forget is that to be separated from God is to be united with Satan. Those are the only two spiritual kingdoms from which we may choose. What does it mean, then, to be united with and separated from God? United is to be part of God's family, to follow God's commandments and traditions. Separated is to be one of His children, to have an identity and free will. That is, we have the best of both!

RUNNING FROM PAIN ·················

What do we do when we see pain coming? If you are like me, you are off and running in the opposite direction. No way do I want to stay around for some painful happening when I can avoid it. There are very few exceptions to this standard operating procedure. I have found that not going to the dentist can be more painful than going periodically, and experiencing just little amounts of pain at a time. Perhaps I will give in to the yearly physical just in case there is something more painful on the horizon. When it comes to exercise, I try very hard to pick those activities which are fun and do not produce pain; there are a number of options available. What is wrong with living a pain-free life?

There is an old cliché, "No pain, no gain." As far as I can remember, each time I wanted to improve my capabilities, there was pain involved. It may be in school classes, on-the-job training, or the old-fashioned trial-and-error method. There was some risk, some pain, some strain, and eventually some gain. So why is it we can not achieve a gain without pain?

I believe it can all be related to change. We live in a changing world and we ourselves are constantly changing. Change is not easy to accommodate. The older we become, the harder it is. The larger the change required, the harder it is. Two years ago I developed a heart condition which required a major change in my lifestyle. That was very painful and, to some extent, still is painful. There are many things I cannot do that I used to do. It is painful to watch other people my age doing all the things which I must now limit myself from. I would like to be with them doing those things.

As another old saying goes, "Pain is inevitable, our response is optional."

So what happens when we can no longer run from pain? That is a major problem in our society. Do we seek diversion in activities, social drugs, or hypnotism to relieve the pressures? Do we go to the psychologist and seek help from mental anguish? Do we go to the doctor to seek drugs that deaden our senses? Or, the ultimate path of escape, do we commit suicide? All the above options are used by many fighting for the right to die when they choose. If the pleasures of life do not outweigh the pain, why should we keep on living?

Is life just a balance between pleasure and pain? If so, how meaningless and valueless life has become. Can it be that the only value in life is pleasure? Is the only thing that keeps us from choosing suicide the fear of dying? What a low state of self-worth we have sunk to. Is that all there is to life?

This is not our Creator's view of life. He considers life a special gift from Him. It comes with His love and concern. It is not our life we are dealing with, it is the life He has given us. If we have a problem in our life, we need to seek His council, guidance and power. Could it be that pain exists in the world to draw us closer to God? It certainly places before us the choice of seeking our own solution or going to God for His guidance. How often I have heard prayers of desperation to God to relieve pain and suffering. How often are these things caused by things we have done? Or, perhaps Satan has attacked us with his fiery darts? In either case, God has allowed the pain and suffering to come into our lives for a purpose—after all, He is in total absolute control! So then, do we ask, "What is God's purpose?" Most likely it has to do with changing our lifestyle and getting back on the path He has set before us. If we can just visualize and accept that, life would take on a whole new meaning. Pain should now be viewed as a signal sent from God to prepare us for change. So, are we waiting in anticipation for the next pain and suffering attack? Well, not quite yet.

Consider the passage,

My son, do not make light of the Lord's discipline, and do not lose heart when he rebukes you, because the Lord disciplines those he loves, and he punishes everyone he accepts as a son (Hebrews 12:6).

Oh, that is hard Scripture. It takes a deep abiding love to discipline those we love; we do not like to hurt them. But in being parents, it is very necessary to punish bad behavior—it is all part of developing self-control in handling our sinful nature. I do hope and pray I can feel God's love just as much as I feel His discipline—then I will be ready.

WHEN LIFE STOPS BEING A MYSTERY ••••••••••

Most people love a mystery. Mystery books are very often bestsellers. TV programming is full of mysteries. Even the regular stories we tell of life are often wrapped in a mystery. The important part about a mystery is that, ultimately, the solution, or the hidden truth it revealed is given, the case is solved. We are totally frustrated if we do not find the answer to the mystery. However, as soon as we find, guess or figure out the mystery, we lose interest. The case is solved, the story written, and the answer given; our interests move on. Let's just face it, life is boring without mystery.

Our drive to conquer mystery is unstoppable. Consider our effort in the sciences to solve the mysteries of life, of our universe and of all creation. We celebrate even the smallest step in unraveling the mysteries. We spend billions upon billions in the exploration of space; what is out there? Great industries have developed for the research, study, teaching and development of resolving the mysteries of health and life. Why do we get sick and why do we die? And even more, how does life begin? One of the areas in which we have made the least progress is in understanding our feelings and emotions; they are mysteries. Psychologists and psychiatrists continue their studies, diagnoses and treatments, but it seems we make little progress. In addition, each new discovery brings with it even more mystery. Will this process ever end?

Perhaps the greatest mysteries are revealed in our religions and their vague concepts of the spiritual world. To resolve these mysteries, many have proposed great systems of doctrine, theology, and traditions. One may ask about the basis for these religions, "Are they anything more than wild human attempts to explain the mystery of life and our existence?" "Are there really any true answers to these mysteries?" Many claim to have the the truth and the answer to life and all of creation, but why, then, are there so many different answers and so many different truths? Can they all be right, as proposed by some? This seems to present even a greater mystery in solving the initial problem. It is more logical that some are closer to the truth and others further away from the truth. So what are we to do? The modernists claim all religions are figments of our imagination, but then proceed to develop their own "religion," which they call their worldview. Like it or not, we all have our own religion, our philosophy of life and purpose which shapes our worldview.

Can we imagine what would happen if the mystery of life and our existence was solved? If all the answers, plots, characters, goals, destinies, procedures, and processes were revealed? All of a sudden God and creation would become boring. It would all be known, and it would be time to go to some other area of mystery and work on the unknown there. However, would there be any mysteries left? The past, the present and the future would all be known. The differences between males and females would all be understood. The conception, birth and development of children would be all predicted and known. The basic result of all this is that we would be gods. What mysteries do gods have? None! (For those of you who have the time and energy, can God create a mystery He cannot solve?).

There must be an answer to all our mysteries! Many give up and accept some form of fatalism; with or without God or gods. Others continue the search, deeper and deeper they go. If it is a false religion, they will eventually come to the end of the mystery. By then, however, it may be too late to begin the quest over again and again. The true infinite mystery will be one not given by humans, but one that is revealed from outside our universe, by the God who created it all. The revelation will confound us, because it must be totally different than our natural thinking and logic—that is the only way it can be an infinite mystery. It must reveal truths of our present universe which we could not deduce on our own, and be based on a domain beyond our existence and abilities to understand. Otherwise, it would not be a real and infinite mystery. The only one I know of is the Great Mystery of God the Father, God the Son and God the Holy Spirit as revealed in the Holy Bible and its Scriptures.

RISING ABOVE THE DAY-TO-DAY ROUTINE •••••

If we are not diligent, we will fall into a monotonous day-to-day routine; each day has its pattern followed by each week, month and year. Is this all we were meant to be? Even the historians follow repeating patterns from decade to decade, century to century and millennia to millennia. What is this driving force to the repeated pattern, a life devoid of adventure, risk and glory? Where is the real meaning in life?

For one thing, there is a natural fear of change, something new and the unknown. It is safe to stay with what we already know and do even though life becomes boring. Also, there really are new dangers in adventuring beyond the borders of our present life. We have to learn new skills, develop new ways of coping with change, and grow to enjoy and relax with new adventures in life. Unfortunately, there is pain, agony and struggle when we face change, especially as we get older. But of what value is living the same day over and over a thousand times?

I am guilty of staying within the lines from day to day. It is so comfortable, relaxing and it has the feeling of being in control. The only excitement and adventure is when something manages to break through from the outside. Then, for a while, confusion, uncertainty and panic prevail. After the turmoil has past, however, there is an exciting tale to tell, a story to write, an adventure that has lifted us beyond the ordinary. Nevertheless, we resent the outside intrusions into our daily lives. If each day were the same, how could we ever tell the passing of time? I have a very set pattern for each day of the week, this is how I can tell time. But I lose track from week to week and month to month.

What is life? A life that just repeats itself day after day is like death. True life is a constant spring of new adventures, we are never to be satisfied with what has been already done. The real joy, happiness and contentment in life come from meeting the challenges of change and overcoming them.

Our God never repeats Himself. Each day is different, each person is different, each animal and plant are different. The clouds in the sky by day and the stars by night are all slightly different; they are in motion. It is only from our passion for control that we want to make things all alike. Cars by the thousands, nails by the millions, and paper by the billions are all as identical as we can make them. Can we imagine a world where every car, nail and piece of paper were different in some way or another? We would be continuously busy trying to figure out how to use them. It is just our nature to make things the same, or at least similar ones in boxes and call them the same.

Our Creator God is always happy with something new and different. The Psalms repeat, *"Sing to the Lord a new song"* at least three times (96:1, 98:1, 149:1). Consider Isaiah 65:17–18:

> *Behold, I will create new heavens and a new earth. The former things will not be remembered, nor will they come to mind. But be glad and rejoice forever in what I will create....*

This is reiterated in Revelation 21:1–4. Our God is constantly doing new things. He expects us to try and do new things as we follow His guidance for our lives.

Perhaps we have difficulty imagining being excited to be in Heaven with God for eternity. What would we do after the first thousand years or so? Would not things begin to get boring? If this is what we may be thinking, we have missed the nature of God. God is infinite, there is no reason for Him to repeat a day or even an hour. There is more than enough creativity for something new and different each hour of eternity. Besides, time will become meaningless in eternity. Scriptures note that, in Heaven, a day is like a thousand years and a thousand years is like a day (Psalm 90:4, 2 Peter 3:8). Obviously we do not grasp the reality of time for eternity and the many dimensions time may have. Equally, we do not understand an infinity of change. But that is exactly what it takes to have a fulfilled life.

A LIFE WITHOUT MEANING ••••••••••••••

What is living a life without meaning? After all, do we not find meaning in everything we do? Is there not meaning in surviving? In eating? In breathing? And reproducing the next generation? Webster's Dictionary describes "meaning" as, 1a. the thing one intends to convey by language (purport), 1b. the thing that is conveyed by language (import), 2. something meant or intended (aim), 3. significant quality, implication of a hidden or special significance, 4a. the logical connotation of a word or phrase, 4b. the logical denotation or extension of a word or phrase. Thus we find two general aspects of meaning—an obvious and natural implication and a hidden and special significance. If we consider the first definition, "a life without meaning" is a meaningless statement as only the existence of life itself has meaning. But meaning from the point of view of purpose, goal and significance— that for most, is a hidden meaning.

For the meaning of "how" we live, we turn to the sciences. For the hidden meaning of "why" we live, we must turn to the theologies. The sciences have a reasonably good track record of passing along the knowledge from one generation to the next. Each generation builds on the knowledge base of the generation before it; the progress over the generations has been outstanding as each generation adds more. However, when we come to the theologies, we find almost exactly the opposite. In place of unifying, focusing and deepening the knowledge base, it is becoming more diverse, dissented, and discouraged. With all this confusion and contention present, even *within* the denominations, it is no wonder many find no significance or meaning to the why of

155

life. Life just is because it is meaningless, purposeless, and detached. How can this be? What has gone wrong in our system? What can bring back meaning?

There are many reasons for how this can be, but one of them is that we try to use the scientific method developed for the physical world to understand the spiritual world. The spiritual laws are nothing like the physical laws we know. A second reason is that there is a major spiritual force trying very hard to confuse our understanding of the spiritual world. That is, there is a spiritual battle in the universe between Satan and his followers and God and his followers. We are caught in the middle—the prizes fought over by these two spiritual powers. God will win, but that will not take place until the end of time, when Satan and his followers are cast out into a far place called Hell. In the meantime, there are many distractions for those who try to find the meaning of life and a relationship with the God of all creation.

Back to our consideration of life without meaning. Many create artificial meanings for life, such as the accumulation of wealth, power, and influence. Others find meaning in their accomplishments and achievements; it is by work that meaning is found. Still others find meaning in the arts; meaning is in the beauty and majesty we see in nature and the creations of our hands. Others find meaning in the survival of life, the fight for dominance, the survival of the fittest and the law of the air, jungle and ocean—eat or be eaten. What type of meaning does this give our lives?

God calls us to a higher meaning for our lives. We are to trust, honor and obey Him; there is no other way to find the true meaning for life. We were created to be His children, members of His family and to reign in Heaven as joint heirs of His Kingdom. We are the Saints of Eternity unbound from the shackles and decay of this present world with its toils, trials and tribulations. Life has new meaning when we come to God asking for forgiveness of our past, and acceptance into His family. This new meaning brings the fruits of the Spirit: love, joy, peace, patience, kindness, goodness faithfulness, gentleness and self-control. For all others, God has set aside a place which extends for eternity, where life has no meaning; it is called Hell. Perhaps not much different then the life many live today, a life without meaning and without end.

LIFE IS NOT FAIR ················

I do not care which way we go about it, life just is not fair. Some begin with more, others receive more and still others end up with more. Where is there justice, equality and righteousness? Nowhere on earth! Governments may try with all their resources to take from the rich and give to the poor, but it never ends up being fair. The rich may give contributions to groups helping the poor, but things never seem to change. Look, hunt and search as I may over these many years, I do not find any place where I would consider life has been fair. Some get far more than they "deserve" and others get far less than they "deserve." Those who have more, generally end up getting more. Those who have less, generally end up losing what they have.

Now, to be completely honest and careful in this analysis, I must admit that I am primarily looking at the outside of everything. Who could say that my judgments are just, equal and right? Each of us would evaluate every situation differently. How could we possibly ever agree on what would be fair? We all rank aspects of life differently—the case of counting apples, oranges and bananas. Not only is life not fair (we can agree on that, somehow), but we cannot agree on what fair would be!

Now let us change our perspective. In place of looking on the "outside" world we live in, let us examine our "inside" world. Ok, how do we do that? We need to get inside a person and examine how they feel, think, believe and respond. There are far more independent dimensions on the inside than on the outside. Furthermore, we have very little control of the outside, and far more control on the inside.

Thus, to be most accurate, it is the inside characteristics we must be evaluating. That is, in place of focusing on how the outside world impacts people, we need to study how the insides of people impact the outside world. Thus, fairness is demonstrated more by how we respond to the outside world than by the world responding to our inside world.

I think we need some examples here. Consider people rich with internal capabilities. That is, those who have self-control, wisdom, knowledge, patience, peace and love. When the outside world attacks them, they are able to maintain their composure and respond in a meaningful way; they can take life's problems in stride.

Now consider someone who has little of these internal capabilities—for one reason or another they have not developed them. When the world attacks them in the same manner as above, they are not able to maintain their composure and respond in a meaningful way. Now, this would be an unfair attack and it should be limited to their ability to respond. If somehow these attacks could be controlled so they were not greater than we could handle with our inside resources, that would be fair. The assumption here is that we are frequently under attack in one way or another. This would be a very different definition of fair, but one in which all could be considered equal. Ok, so how do we control these attacks?

The answer is God. If we accept God's Son, Jesus Christ, as our Lord and Saviour, He will make sure the attacks from the outside world will not overcome us. In that way, life will be fair. Furthermore, He does this in such a way as to allow us to develop our internal strengths. If we are to grow, then we need the continuing attacks from the outside world—no attacks, no growth. Interesting!

It just so happens we live in Satan's domain on earth, as the Bible describes. Satan is constantly on the attack, seeking out those he can destroy or dominate, that is, attack them with greater strength than their internal resources. As such, we must consider Satan very unfair in his ways. He is deceitful, cunning and out to control us. Our only defenses are God's spiritual armor which protects us from being over-come by Satan. But is this whole scene fair?

The earth is a battleground of good versus evil; we either learn to be good children of God with His guiding protec-tion, or fall pray to Satan's ways. However, this is not the End! God has prepared a new Heaven and a new Earth where Satan and all his followers will be cast out and far removed into a place called Hell. In this new environment, there will be no more suffering , sickness and death—that is, no more attacks by Satan to destroy us. It will be fair on the inside and outside! God has promised that goodness, righteousness and fairness will prevail.

ONE QUARTER OF THE CIRCLE, PLEASE! ·······

Many times I do not want the whole piece, but just part. When I was young and wild, I would carefully analyze just what needed to be done in any given situation, and only do that much. When I took a girl out on a date, I would only wash the part of the car that she would see—the right-hand side and the hood. That saved a lot of time. When painting a room, not all the walls and woodwork can be seen. It is very, very tempting to only paint the part someone will see. I think the best example of this principle is Hollywood and their movies— they only build the front of the buildings and change sizes to show distance and height. At Disney World's MGM studio area, this is easy to see, but the set looks very real on the movies. Such is the mind I have to work with; it only wants to work on the outside image someone may see, and not complete the whole circle inside and out. A quarter of the circle, please.

Not everything can be divided into pieces. For example, a quarter of the circle does not give us a smaller circle; it produces only a section of an arc, which is not a circle. If we were trying to use this quarter circle as a smaller wheel, it would not work at all. On the other hand, a quarter pound of coffee is quite useful in brewing coffee, as we very seldom make enough coffee at the same time to use a whole bag. I have seen this quarter principle misused in approaching the Bible and God. Why can't one have just quarter of the Bible and a quarter of God? In doing this, we can end up with a smaller set of writings and a smaller god, both which that are compatible with us. What is wrong with this?

Why can't we pick and choose the passages of the Bible and the characteristics of God we want to incorporate into our lives? We just want the parts we can understand and which fit comfortably in our life; the rest just does not meet our needs! Obviously, there are some ramifications when we do this. What I think of first is, who is in control? If we are doing the picking and choosing, we are in control. Only those changes we approve will be made. If we accept the whole Bible and the whole God, then God would be picking and choosing the changes in our lives He wanted to make. This definitely would be more affective and challenging then we would designate. Why should we give up our control?

Consider going to a doctor to cure a serious problem we have. After listening to the doctor, we might pick and choose only parts of his recommendations that we like. Most likely we will not get healed and we may even get worse. For healing to take place, the whole procedure must be endured; all the elements of the medical procedure are interconnected. Selecting and choosing breaks this synergism and only a partial effect is achieved at best. But how does this apply to the Bible and God? We are not going to them because we are seriously sick and need healing; all we need is a little up-lift or a quick answer to prayer! Really?

The Bible declares we are spiritually sick unto death because of all our sins. We have rebelled against God and the penalty for this is eternal separation and Hell—the spiritual death. But we do not feel spiritually sick and as though we are dying! That is a problem because we do not know what full spiritual health is like. We were born with a sinful nature and have been going down hill spiritually, ever since. The Scriptures describe spiritual health as having *"love, joy, peace, patience, kindness, goodness, faithfulness, gentleness and self-control."* (Galatians 5:22–23). The cure for spiritual sickness and death is very strict; there is only one way to be healed and we must take the full treatment—no quarter portion of a cure will do. We must repent of our rebellion against God and accept His Son, Jesus Christ, as our Lord and Saviour, and follow His direction for our lives. Further,

> *All Scripture is God-breathed and is useful for teaching, rebuking, correction and training in righteousness, so that the man of God may be thoroughly equipped for every good work* (2 Timothy 3:16).

There are some thirty passages in the New Testament discussing the fulfillment of the Scriptures. Jesus rebuked Satan using the Scriptures. They are powerful truths of God to be used in our lives. Consider what Jesus said, *"Heaven and earth will pass away, but my words will never pass away."* (Matthew 24:35). God's Word is eternal, absolute truth. It does not work for us to pick and choose the quarter of the circle of God's Word to guild our lives, we must include all of Scripture and all of God to have an abundant eternal fulfilled life.

THE NATURAL AND THE ARTIFICIAL ••••••••••••

Who would want the artificial when they can have the natural? So goes a new wave of thinking in our society. In making this choice—choosing the natural and throwing out the artificial—we are actually making things much worse for ourselves and future generations. This movement may be recognized as the Mother earth movement (environmentalism movements), or as the progressivism in education, just to mention two. The attraction seems to be the underlying romanticism of going back to the natural methods and techniques. It follows the previous idea, "Stop the World, I want to get off." Technology is developing too fast, change is taking place too often, and we are running out of time and space. Let's all go back to Nature and live in the forests where life is real and simple.

There are many hidden problems in the assumption that the natural is the best. For example, math is artificial, we created it out of a logical need to be quantitative and qualitative about our observations. Math is a powerful tool which provides the basis for our sciences and technology growth. Consider languages—they are also artificial. We developed arbitrary symbols to represent an alphabet from which we make up words and assign to them meanings. This way we can communicate, express our ideas and develop a knowledge base. Next there are anesthesia, vaccinations, and medicines to prevent illnesses and to help us recover from illness and accidents when they happen. Most of these are artificial processes and products. Without these, our life expectancy would be much shorter, not to mention our standard of living lower. For many, our mainline religions are artificial, that is, unlike worshiping the earth or the animals and spirits of the earth. God is not something or someone that is natural in our environment; God is artificial from the physical world's perspective. Thus, a change in viewpoint should be made there also.

The impact of this naturalism undercurrent will surface in many areas with major conflicts in society's forecast for the future. The basic tenets of naturalism are impervious to logic, reason and even testing, as these, too, are artificial, and therefore not to be considered. The only things that are true and real are those which are natural. It is hard to understand how this romanticism has impacted so many people's thinking. But that is probably the point, it is an escape from logic and reason. It is a movement that I believe could take us back to the Dark Ages. The basis of our present civilization would be torn apart by this thinking. The education of our children would be turned away from the sciences and technology; this is of great concern to many presently evaluating our school system. As for religion, change-over to a secular theology will have many ramifications. Romanticism is a secularized expression of religious faith, the natural divinity of this world.

If people put their faith in this world, they are doomed to failure. It is like putting our faith in a machine—our car for example. Most of the time it works, but when it doesn't, we are without alternatives as many of us do not know how things work and cannot fix them. It will become old, wear out, and need to be replaced. The question is, "Will these people live long enough to realize this?" Since their ears do not respond to logic and reason, only the impact of the environment can be their teachers. That, they will not understand without the background and technology of the sciences. Nature's lessons are hard and fast without compassion or remorse.

Even the Bible discusses the change to romanticism in several ways. In 2 Timothy 4:3–4,

For the time will come when men will not put up with sound doctrine. Instead, to suit their own desires, they will gather around them a great number of teachers to say what their itching ears want to hear. They will turn their ears away from the truth and turn aside to myths.

Saint Paul wrote:

For although they knew God, they neither glorified him as God nor gave thanks to him, but their thinking became futile and their foolish hearts were darkened. Although they claimed to be wise, they became fools and exchanged the glory of the immortal God for images made to look like mortal man and birds and animals and reptiles… They exchanged the truth of God for a lie, and served created things rather than the Creator—who is forever praised. Amen (Romans 1:21–23,25).

In many passages, such as Matthew 11:15, Jesus Christ is quoted as saying, *"He who has ears to hear, let him hear."* Since God is the Creator, if anything is natural and real, it is God, and if anything is artificial and temporal, it would be His creation. I think they have the whole thing backwards!

THE K.I.S.S. SYNDROME ··············

I have long been an advocate of the "Keep It Simple, Stupid" philosophy, but perhaps from a different perspective than the norm. If one really knows their subject in depth, they are able to give a very simple explanation or analogy. However, the novice is most apt to make the explanation far more complex than necessary because they, themselves, are not all that clear on the subject. There is a second misuse of the K.I.S.S. approach, that is, taking something very complex and simplifying it to the point where it can be easily grasped, but thus becomes completely inaccurate and misleading.

An example of the first misuse of K.I.S.S. is a news reporter trying to explain Einstein's General Theory of Relativity, which has recently become news because of the discovery of the Cosmology Constant by astrophysicists. This is a condition where the gravitational forces are being counteracted by unknown forces related to the Cosmology Constant, so that expansion of the universe is not slowing down as has been predicted. Now, there is a lot more that can be said, but for the general public, it will not add to the understanding of the basic discovery.

An example of the second kind is the reports from politicians on Global Warming; we are burning more fossil fuel, therefore there is more CO_2 in the air, which causes Global Warming. In actuality, however, we have been in a mini-ice age, cooling for the last several hundred years and we're just getting more back to normal temperature. The satellite data does not confirm a Global Warming, but the temperatures of weather stations, generally in cities and at airports where there are lots of paving and heat-absorbing materials, do show

167

a slight trend for heating, more near the poles than at the equator. Also, historical accounts of global temperature have shown significant new developments, more food production and better health when the world had warmer temperatures. The subject of Global Warming is far more complex than the burning of fossil fuels.

I believe there to be a third misuse of K.I.S.S. in our schools—that is, in keeping school simple, we are excluding many valuable subjects. We live in an increasingly complex society and world. The many sciences are having major impacts on the world and all our lives, but it is not emphasized in our schools, especially in our colleges for the liberal arts graduates. Other major areas generally not emphasized are the philosophies, in which I include political "science," sociology, and religion, as well as philosophy. These are the areas that have to do with how people interact, and the meaning of life. Then there are the communications skills of reading, writing, speaking, languages, and the arts with music, drama, and painting/sculpture. Last, but not least, are the practical skills in homemaking and, for a few, the trade professions, with wood shop, metal shop, electrical/ electronic shop, auto shop, computer labs, economics including taxes, cooking classes and gardening/farming. Where have all these gone?

The fourth area of concern is the implementation of K.I.S.S. in our churches and religions. Many of those attending church are basically illiterate when it comes to Biblical knowledge and background. In many cases, I believe pastors and teachers have kept their teaching too simple and therefore have not challenged members. The point of the Christian life is a relationship with Jesus Christ; the concept is very simple but the implementation, incredibly complex. Let us consider the K.I.S.S. advice in the Bible, in the Book of Proverbs, mostly written by Solomon, a man of great wisdom and knowledge:

"A simple man believes anything, but a prudent man gives thought to his steps" (14:15).

"The simple inherit folly, but the prudent are crowned with knowledge" (14:18).

"How much better to get wisdom than gold, to choose understanding rather than silver!" (16:16).

"Folly delights a man who lacks judgment, but a man of understanding keeps a straight course (15:21)

"When words are many, sin is not absent, but he who holds his tongue is wise" (10:19).

"He who trusts in himself is a fool, but he who walks in wisdom is kept safe" (28:26).

"The fear of the Lord teaches a man wisdom, and humility comes before honor" (15:33).

So, it is not that K.I.S.S. is a bad concept, but that it must be applied correctly and under the proper circumstances, with wisdom. There are many who enjoy the one-liners, but never go any deeper. This is the pit-fall. And when applied to our understanding of God, it can become the K.I.S.S. of spiritual death.

THE WORLDVIEW CENTERS ···············

Where do we go to find our worldview? Do we watch, listen and read the various news and entertainment media sources? Is it from the business and finance world? Could it be the academic institutions and colleges? Or perhaps our social groups and clubs? Maybe even our church, synagogue, temple, or mosque? Perhaps we may even try to mix them all together. There are many choices for our own personal Worldview Center.

Most likely we go shopping at the various centers picking up bits and pieces here and there and, in our spare time, assembling them into our Grand Worldview. In the process, it would be expected that each and every one of us will have a different worldview. This being the case, how do we ever come to any agreements? Fortunately we have strong, medium and weak worldviews, depending upon the subject and application, so there is room for negotiations and com-promises. I doubt if we every spend much time regarding the medium and weak views; it the the strong ones we are out to defend and protect. Thus, the obvious question is, "Where is the source for our strong worldviews?" Which Center do we elect for the pivotal positions?"

Our choices are based on our priorities; what comes first? In my education years, it was my parents, school and the church. At this time the rest of the world was insignificant. In my working years it was academics, businesses, and the church all in second position, as I had to support my family and all their needs. Now, in my retirement years it is the church and academics, with finances secondary.

This is not necessarily the model for everyone. Problems arise when our worldviews are strongly divergent and there is no room for compromise. Anyone who holds a worldview assuming it is the only right position brings grief to many.

We have reached a condition in our societies where many groups have adopted a worldview they hold as the only true one; all other viewpoints are wrong, destructive and must be abolished. The time is long overdue for One-World Order, the Unified Worldview. Our world has long been searching for this One-World Order. We have many world wars in the attempt to have one dominating worldview. It would appear we have another one growing from the Islam religion, primarily from the fundamental extremists. In place of the conventional all-out military assault, they have chosen terrorism, because of their very limited force in a direct attack. Their goal is the same—for all people to believe what they do, and to destroy those who don't. Is there any other possible outcome for our world civilization? That is, must the battles over worldviews be fought in each generation? Is there any other solution possible?

Let us consider the Christian worldview as presented in the Holy Bible. One of the main points of the Bible is that the final battle will not be fought on earth, but in the spiritual domains, by God and His angels. The good news is that He has already won! Satan and his deceivers have been defeated. Second, the true creation of the New World Order will take place on the Great White Throne on Judgment Day. Those who have committed themselves to God's Son, Jesus, will be present with Him for eternity in Heaven. Those who have chosen other worldviews will be cast into Hell and given a World Order of eternal torment. This is not a war Christians are to be involved in on earth or in Heaven; we do not have the resources, the knowledge or the power to fight. As Christians, however, we are involved in the war of truth; the war of ideas, priorities, and values. We are to present Christianity, the personal relationship with Jesus Christ, as our worldview. It is not our role to make this happen, but we are to pray and follow the leading of the Holy Spirit. It is the Holy Spirit who moves to change the hearts of people and to accept God's true Worldview Center. All other positions seek to elevate man as god, and for man to rule as a god. This is exactly what Satan tried to do—take over God's Kingdom. Now, Satan and his followers seek to have humans follow his worldview and set up a New World Order under him on our earth.

....

CHAPTER 3

Physical and Spiritual Theology Pondered

I enjoy reading the Bible, but I have a hard time understanding it. It is a struggle to figure out its meaning for my life. Thus, as I work my way through the various questions raised by Scriptures, I find great help in writing down my thoughts and conclusions. I share these with the reader that they may help in the understanding of the Bible.

Whilst you are divided betwixt God and the world, you have neither the pleasures of Religion, nor the pleasures of the world, but are always in the uneasiness of a divided heart. You have only so much Religion as serves to disquiet you, to show you a handwriting on the wall, to interrupt your pleasures, and to appear as a death's-head at all your feasts, but not Religion enough to give you a taste and feeling of its pleasures. You dare not wholly neglect Religion, but then you take no more than is just sufficient to keep you from being a terror to yourself, and you are as loth to be very good as you are fearful to be very bad.

William Law (1686–1761)

DO WE KNOW GOD? ···············

Everyone has some opinion or thought about God; who He is, what He is, why He is and where He is. I would have thought by now that we should have figured it all out, but a lot of confusion remains ; just consider the following definitions:

"Love."	The Bible
"A superior reasoning power... revealed in the incomprehensible universe."	Albert Einstein
"Conscience."	Mohandas Gandhi
"A light that is never darkened."	Francis Quarles
"A mighty fortress."	Martin Luther
"Personified incomprehensibility."	George Lichtenberg
"That which has no definition."	Joseph Albo
"A vengeful, pitiless, and almighty fiend."	Percy Bysshe Shelly
"An infantile fantasy... necessary when men did not know what lightning was."	Edward Anhalt
"A gaseous vertebrate."	Earnst Haeckel
"Father."	Jesus Christ

This list reveals the great diversity in opinions of God. Now it would seem logical that a mature person should not give a definition of God unless they truly know God. Thus, is it possible all these definitions are valid?

Yes, these are all quite possible definitions, because different people have different relationships with God and God has different relationships with people. Scripture reveals God's different relationships with two people, *"Yet I have loved Jacob, but Esau I have hated ... "* (Malachi 1: 2). Thus two people may have opposite views of God, depending upon their relationship with Him. From these two extremes, the possibilities for all in-between relationships exists. If someone says, "God is an infantile fantasy...," for him that is most likely very true, for that reflects his relationship with God. It does stretch one's imagination and understanding to accept that different relationships with God are possible.

Further note, Jesus asked,

> *"Who do people say the Son of Man is?" They replied, "Some say John the Baptist; other say Elijah; and still other Jeremiah or one of the prophets." "But what about you?" he asked. "Who do you say I am?" Simon Peter answered, "You are the Christ, the Son of the living God." Jesus replied, "Blessed are you, Simon son of Jonah, for this was not revealed to you by man, but my my Father in heaven"* (Matthew 16:15–17).

What do we conclude from this discussion about knowing God? If our knowledge of God is from people, we know God only as their relationships reflect. If we know God through the inspirations of the Holy Spirit, we then have a revelation from God Himself, which goes far beyond any relationship we may have with people—good or bad.

There remains one basic problem. The words and thoughts we communicate with others are limited to our worldly experiences and conditions. To explain a relationship outside this world to a person who has not experienced such relationship would be impossible or, at best, result in a very distorted misunderstanding. Thus, we must test the secular and spiritual content of any response to the question, "Do we know God?" Is this answer a secular one or a spiritual one, or both? In a practical sense, I think this will be very difficult to determine. Many can do the spiritual talk who do not have the spiritual walk. It is more the nature of who we are than what we say, that answers the question, "Do we know God?" If we truly know God, we will either be like God's children and love God, or be like Satan and his children and hate God. For those with only a worldly view of God, the answers will range greatly in the wide relationship spectrum.

BELIEVING IN GOD ···············

Statistics show that eighty percent of the people living in the United States believe in God. The general interpretation is that eighty percent of the people believe there is *a* god. This is partly because of our cultural conditioning and the traditions of the founding fathers of our country. Even our currency states, "IN GOD WE TRUST." Most everyone is satisfied with this statement, as long as we don't go any further than the generic definition for "god." In this way we have a general unity in belief in a god.

Should someone be more specific, however, and carefully define who they believe their god to be and what he does; we now have unresolvable conflicts. This poses a most interesting paradox. If we really know God and have a relationship with Him, we all would have the very same general definitions of the character, nature and abilities of God. If not, we could conclude that there are many gods, perhaps even one god for each person—our own personal god. Some will insist that it is impossible to know god, that he is far beyond us and does not choose to communicate with us in any personal way. Thus we are forever limited to believing in a remote, impersonal, powerful being who has removed himself (herself or itself) from us and we will never ever really know this god.

It comes as a shock to many to find that the Christian God, as revealed in Scriptures, wants to have a very personal and intimate relationship with His created people. Not only this, but God's Son, Jesus came to earth and took on the form of a man and lived among us. In this way, Jesus was able to have personal relationships with people, one-on-one, and reveal His true personality, purpose and power. At the time Jesus walked on the earth, there was no confusion about His characteristics or what He did; the issue was whether or not He was God. In those times, many could not believe that any god would want to have direct relationships with all humans—perhaps with a few of the very elite religious leaders, but certainly not with all the common folk! That was not the god they believed in!

Furthermore, how would it even be possible for God to have relationships with everyone? We, ourselves, have difficulties with more than a few people—at best, a few hundred people—but billions of people? Impossible! However, Scripture notes, *He determines the number of the stars and calls them each by name* (Psalm 147:4). Now, consider the present estimate of stars in our universe is a thousand, billion, billion (1×10^{21})—far more than the number of people who have ever lived. Thus, the issue of God's relationships with us should not be a matter of numbers, but of the most supreme being lowering Himself to associate with us common folk. That just is not done in our society; we must stay in our places and with our type of people. Scripture states that, in God's eyes, we are all equal. There are also comments about how God takes care of the birds in the field and the lilies that bloom in such beautiful array.

Perhaps we are mixing our worlds? Our world is controlled by Satan. The responses we see in our culture and nature are due to Satan's influence and control. Thus, if we formulate our god based on the conditions and traditions of our society, we are most likely creating Satan as our god. The "human" characteristics we have to rebel against God are those caused by Satan's temptations back in the early history of humankind. To project those onto a god is to come up with a fallen god, which is essentially Satan's history; he was the highest of the angels, the created beings of God. He tried to be God, but was cast down to earth and given this kingdom to rule.

However, we are created beings in the image of God, not to be confused with our present fallen nature. Thus, to develop a culture and nature which reflects our God in Heaven, we must study God's Kingdom. By careful study of the Scriptures, we can develop a new model of God's Kingdom. From these characteristics, we will also develop a totally different model of God. We also have the example of God's Son, Jesus, when He was on earth. Jesus taught about both the Kingdom of God and the nature of God. With these insights, we cannot confuse the two worlds of our existence. Thus we have two bases for developing our belief in God— one, Satan's nature of deception, lies, and secrecy, the other, the Kingdom of God, Jesus and the Scriptures, which reflects a nature of love, mercy, peace, joy and openness.

GOD IS NOT A MAN! ···············

It is obvious that God is not a man, just look at creation. This was not designed, built and operated by a man! Men would do things much differently. We would have light or dark, not this long transition period of twilight in between. And what is with all the flowers? They serve no practical purpose and waste a lot of the plants' energy. If God wanted to make a plant for man, I suggest a Beer Tree, one whose fruit contains cool beer. The planets are too far away to be usable; they should be closer so we could use them as stepping stones in space. Besides, it does not appear they are hospitable environments to live in. The stars make good reference points at night, but there are too many of them. They should be a little brighter and spaced at regular intervals. In fact, if they were quite a bit brighter we would not have any night, and thus no reason to sleep. We could work all day and all night. Sleep is a real time-waster and nothing gets accomplished. There are lots of areas where the universe could be more practical, useful and efficient.

When we come to man himself, there are some limitations that should not be. Why is man not the strongest animal on earth? How can he possibly be in control when he is not physically superior to all other animals? Why can't man fly? If the birds can do it, then man should be able to do it. While we are at it, we should be able to breathe underwater like the fish do. Why is the whale so big? That "fish" makes man look so small and insignificant! I think man should be at least twenty-five feet tall. That way we could do a lot more things and not need a ladder. I even would like eyes in the back of my head and perhaps one on top. I don't want to be surprised by someone coming from behind or from above. It would save a lot of time turning around not to mention bumping into things that are too low. We could design hats with eye holes and shades....

Now let's consider woman. The Bible notes that the woman is a helpmate for man. Well, I think God got that wrong, too. If God understood men, he would have made women differently. To most everything I want to do, my wife says, "You should not do that!" What kind of a helpmate is that? She is all concerned and bothered about things that do not seem very important to me. Worse than that, I cannot figure her out. She has a logic that defies logic!

So, I place my case before you: God is not a man! Ok, if God is not a man, who is God? The Bible keeps referring to "Him." We have God the Father and God the Son. Both of those we would normally assume to be men. Then, God the Holy Spirit. Don't know how we are going to classify that One… the Holy Spirit, He? My assumption is that the cultural norm is to refer to God as "He." The image of man is one of power, authority and control. God, the Trinity, certainly has all the power, authority and control. However, the Bible also says God has love, mercy and grace. To my way of thinking, these are more feminine characteristics. If we are to put these together, we should be referring to God as He-She… or is that She-He? This could explain why I have so many problems always trying to think of God as He.

I need to be careful about this, because if God did not have love, mercy and grace, I would be in big trouble. I need God's love, mercy and grace every day. As hard as I may try, I cannot live a perfect life; even for one day, or is it one hour? I continually need God's forgiveness and encouragement to keep going, to keep trying.

Another thing. This world and the universe we zip around in would be quite a boring place if it did not have beauty, inspiration and wonder. Let's not forget the mystery! There is no way to figure everything out in a lifetime, or, for a matter of fact, thousands, maybe even billions of lifetimes. There is an unfathomable depth and breadth to our universe that surpasses all our knowledge, wisdom and abilities, something only an infinite God could Create. If God is infinite, then God is beyond both men and women, beyond the He-She or She-He. Thus, we may also conclude that God is not She either. God is beyond dimension, definition and gender.

THE CROSS ················

The Cross stands at the end of Jesus' life, the culmination of His mission on earth. Do we fully understand what it means for Jesus Christ to give up His life so that we may be set free from the burden and penalty of sin? How can we? We have trouble understanding the judgment of sin. To break God's commandments by deed is one thing, but Jesus expanded the meaning to include both thought and deed. Who could possibly live to such high standards? Our failure was inevitable. Can this all be caused by our sinful nature inherited from Adam and Eve?

If God's grace abounds in forgiving of all our sins, why stop sinning? Also, why wouldn't everyone be saved? As long as Jesus paid for all our sins, everyone would be covered by God's grace. However, this is not what the Scriptures state; grace is available to all, but only given to those who accept Jesus Christ as their Lord and Saviour. Furthermore, we talk about our free will, but Scriptures note that we were chosen before the beginning of time. In a sense, we are predestined. Where is our free will in all this? We certainly have a free will to sin; is this all predestined too?

At the Cross, Jesus gave up His life to pay for our sins; His eternal life was separated from God when He was temporarily cast into Hell. Now how many "lives" did Jesus Christ have? We know He had His human life, and that one He gave up in death. But what about His God life, that is, His eternal life? If it is eternal life, how could He have given it up? Besides, the Scriptures note He spent three days in the heart of the earth (Hell?), which would imply He was not totally dead and gone. (How do three days pay for our eternity in Hell?), for on the third day, He was resurrected. Which life is that? One assumes His human life. He then left earth to join His Father at His right hand in Heaven. This is the spiritual domain, which requires a spiritual life. What we have here is very confusing and does not fit any of our worldly experiences.

How might we find some basis of understanding of what is going on and what it might mean? Certainly in our four-dimensional world of height, width, length and time, we have no way of understanding how this all may be. Thus, we assume there must be something more, but what? As mentioned before, there is new insight from the latest discoveries in the astro-physics and cosmology fields of science. The present theory is that our universe really has eleven dimensions, if not more. This is a requirement for the combination of the Gravitational Theory with the General Theory of Relativity and the Super String Theory, all necessary for the initial phases of the creation of the universe—"The Big Bang." These seven (or more) other dimensions are curled about our present four dimensions of space and time. This makes possible the smoothing transition between all the dimensions. To appear in our four dimensions requires only moving from the seven higher dimensions into our four-dimensional space and time, like walking through a door. The existence of higher dimensionality gives us a potential physical model of what the Scriptures may be talking about when referring to Jesus' human, yet divine life.

We can propose that our eternal life exists somewhere in these higher seven dimensions but, at present, we are blinded to these dimensions and banned from make the transition. This dimensional limitation could also be related to the judgments of God on Adam and Eve for their sins. Being limited to just the four space and time dimensions, we would surely die like everything else in this world, and being stuck in the lower part of the eleven dimensions in eternal life may also exclude us from Heaven.

We can now propose that when Jesus died he left our four dimensions and existed in the seven other dimensions but, due to taking on all our sins, was banned from Heaven and sent to the "heart of the earth" to await judgment. After three days—our time scale, it could be much longer in other time dimensions—God accepted Jesus' death on the Cross as payment for all our sins, and resurrected Him back to our four dimensions. After a short time on earth, Jesus transitioned out of our four dimensions and into the seven other dimensions to be with God in Heaven. Because of the direct interaction possible between all of these eleven dimensions, free will, predestination, time and even sin have very fluid meanings. This dimensional model varies from the more traditional one of the kingdom of earth and Kingdom of Heaven, in that the interactions of these kingdoms are not defined. In the physical eleven-dimensional universe, these interactions are basically defined and total interaction is possible. Regarding the creation process, God's Kingdom would be expected to have even higher dimensions, from which these eleven were chosen. Each increasing level of dimension would represent higher power and authority.

GOOD AND EVIL ················

There are several basic problems in trying to distinguish between good and evil. The first is the definition of "good." For example, we talk about good and bad. This is not the same as good and evil. For example, if I can come down with the flu, that is bad, but it is not evil. Or I can get up in the morning feeling good, but that is not the same "good" with regards to good and evil. I propose that the phrase should really be Holy and Evil, to try and distinguish the different meanings of "good" in good and evil, versus good and bad.

Philosophers have struggled over the definition of "good," as do the writers of dictionaries. The first step is to distinguish between the use of "good" as an adjective, as in "good, better, best," and as a noun. In this essay, "good" is used as a noun. Now, there are several categories of good. Webster's Dictionary gives the following: 1a: something that is good; b: conforming to the moral order of the universe or praiseworthy character; c: good element or portion; 2: prosper or benefit for the community; 3a: something that has economic utility or satisfies economic wants, b: personal property that has intrinsic value; c: cloth, d: wares, commodities or merchandise; 4: good person; 5: plural-proof of wrongdoing. Are we confused yet? The problem is that "good" is over-used, and has too many meanings.

There are two basic competing philosophies of life in our Western world—one believes there is no God and one believes there is a God, the difference between all that is relative, conditional and probable, and absolute truth, moral law and eternal judgment. The philosophies say "Without

God, there is only Good and Bad, but with God there is Holy and Evil, along with Good and Bad." How can this be?

Without God, how can there be holy and evil? Webster's does not provide a clear distinction between good and holy or between bad and evil. These definitions overlap. Thus, the relationship between the terms must be considered in the light of an existent and non-existent God. This would argue "good" and "bad" as elements of the physical world, and "holy" and "evil" as elements of the spiritual world. It is true that we have great difficulty, in many cases, distinguishing between physical and spiritual manifestations; this is perhaps the basis of confusion with word definitions. Things can get further complicated when God works within someone for them to do good, which could also be holy, and, conversely, when Satan tempts, deceives or motivates someone to do bad things, which could also be evil. Thus, we may find physical deeds as good or bad depending upon the motivations, which may have been holy or evil.

The only way out of this dilemma of definitions, I find, is through the Scriptures. For example:

"And we know that in all things God works for the good of those who love him, who have been called according to his purpose" (Romans 8:28). God is able to take a short-term "bad" and turn it into a long-term "good," to take "evil" and turn it into the "holy."

"Your enemy the devil prowls around like a roaring lion looking for someone to devour" (1 Peter 5:8). Evil waits at our doorstep to pull us down; to get us to do bad and evil things.

"For what I do is not the good I want to do; no, the evil I do not want to do—this I keep on doing" (Romans 7:19). We have a sinful nature that pulls us down, but we know that God's

Laws are spiritual and good (holy). Good and bad, holy and evil are constantly at war.

> *Do not be anxious about anything, but in everything, by prayer and petition, with thanksgiving, present your requests to God. And the peace of God, which transcends all understanding, will guard you hearts and your minds in Christ Jesus* (Philippians 4:6–7).

We are not able of our own strength to win the battle of good versus bad and holy versus evil. However, through prayer, praise and petition to our Holy Father we can receive the strength and direction to be faithful to His will for our lives.

EVIL IS ALL AROUND US ················

I have put up a fence around our property with controlled gates, but still evil comes in. We have a very efficient police force that is on duty twenty-four hours a day and seven days a week; still evil gets in. We are a country of laws to eliminate evil and have a judicial system to enforce them; still evil gets loose. We have the best military force in the world to protect us from evil; still evil attack. What is this evil we seem powerless to control?

On September 11, 2001 the forces of evil prevailed in a most devastating and traumatic way on the World Trade Center and, to a lesser degree, on the Pentagon. We will never be the same. If we look at the animal life or plant life or even the devastation of nature in fire, floods and ground-moving forces we do not see evil, but a natural evolution following well-established laws of nature. In part, these are the forces of survival, the forces of aging, and the forces of ecology. These forces are not intentionally evil; they renew the earth for life to continue. If nature is not the source of evil, what is?

We see evil played out in the acts and deeds of mankind. If this evil does not come from natural sources, it must come from supernatural sources strong enough to overcome our built-up defenses against it. It is like a force that takes over a person and changes them from a human to an inhuman being, diabolically against fellow human beings. This is a force that is totally destructive, with no redeeming graces; it possesses a passion so great that the affected people's own lives are insignificant. Their only purpose is to destroy anything and everything that is in their way. What is the source of this great evil?

If one had no other reason to believe in the Bible, its account of the evil that has entered the human race should be sufficient. There is a war going on between good and evil, between God and Satan. Satan has rebelled against God and is out to destroy all God has created, especially God's highest creation, human beings. This is not a physical but a spiritual battle, one in which Satan is out to control as many humans as he can and turn them into forces of evil. Satan is very powerful and intelligent, with an army of demons to help him. He is the source of deception, lies and death. He seeks to destroy all mankind's achievements, especially those which honor and worship God. What chance do we have against Satan's forces?

God is more powerful, more intelligent, and more knowing than Satan and all his forces. If God is for us, who can be against us? We must put on the full armor of God to protect us from the attacks of Satan. This is not physical, but spiritual armor that provides our defense. We must learn to fight spiritual battles, for that is where, through our Saviour Jesus Christ, we win the victory . If we just rely on our physical strength and resources, we will not survive, for Satan's physical forces are far stronger then we are.

The battle is not over until the end of time and we come to the Great White Throne Judgement. Many have asked and prayed that Satan and all his evil be removed from our world so that we can live in peace. However, God has higher purposes for continuing this battle with evil. Is it perhaps through evil that we seek, find and depend upon God? Is it perhaps part of the testing we go through to develop our spirit and soul? Is evil perhaps a way through which God can reveal His great power, love and mercy for us? Is it perhaps due to our inherited fallen nature? Is evil part of the great drama of life, that which gives it meaning and purpose? Is it that part of the many dimensions of creation, some seen and some unseen, allow, and perhaps require, Satan and his evil to continue to exist? Regardless, we have been given a way to escape Satan's evil temptations and the judgments of God through Jesus Christ and the power of the Cross. By accepting Jesus as our Lord and Saviour, our past transgressions can be forgiven and we can become Children of God for eternity with Him in Heaven.

TERRORISM—A SPIRITUAL BATTLE ·············

The terrorist attack on the twin towers of the World Trade Center was a physical act in carrying out a spiritual battle. Most of the comments and discussions I have heard or read deal only with the physical aspects of this threat; there is more. We are in a spiritual battle. Let us examine the spiritual aspects of this battle against terrorism.

As we listen to the rhetoric of Osama bin Laden, do we focus on the physical or the spiritual threats? He is calling this a Holy War of Islam against the United States of America and all who support our way of life. Most often we probably disregard the religious aspects as just more radical thinking of another fanatic. Is he just using the Islam religion to reach his political ambitions? Many may conclude there is nothing spiritual behind this at all. I have a different perspective.

Since the beginning of time our world has been the battleground between Satan and God. We pick up the story in Genesis with Satan tempting and deceiving Adam and Eve. The temptation has continued since. Satan is the active organizer, the spiritual source of evil. Terrorism does produce physical effects, but its source is spiritual. Thus, if we only fight terrorism with physical force, we are attacking only the agents of Satan and not the source. If we fight with spiritual forces, we directly attack Satan and his agents, before the terrorist acts have taken place. Yes, there is a spiritual battle, even after the terrorist attacks in rebuilding the body, soul and spirit.

Consider the Scriptures,

If my people, who are called by my name, will humble themselves and pray and seek my face and turn from their

193

wicked ways, then will I hear from heaven and will forgive their sin and will heal their land (2 Chronicles 7:14).

This follows the passage in which God allows disasters to fall on the land. Whether it be drought, desolation, plagues or terrorists, God is able to heal our land. However, it requires a spiritual awakening, repenting and turning back to God. In the history of early Israel, Jews fell way from God and went after other gods. Disaster would come upon them. As a result, they would slowly turn back to God and things would become good again. This cycle went on many times. It is as though each generation has to learn the hard way that God is Lord and in control of all.

So what are we doing about terrorism? Do we build up our defenses and offenses to protect ourselves? Certainly we have let our military dwindle down to a low state of readiness, because we did not see any significant threats. Now we have threats! It is right and reasonable to build up our military capabilities. However, we also need to build up our spiritual defenses and offenses. They, too, have fallen into disrepair and need major reinforcements. This is a personal responsibility for each Christian—the call to spiritual arms. Put on the full armor of God and be active in prayer, attacking the evil of this world. Together with God we stand, but divided from Him we fall.

THE SEDUCTIVE POWER OF EVIL ···············

If someone gets angry and shouts at me, I generally respond by getting angry and shouting back at them. If someone pushes me, I most likely will push them back. If someone hits me, my self-defense is to hit them back. If someone were to shoot a gun at me, I would respond by shooting back at them if I had a gun. The natural response to an evil act is to do similar evil acts, if not worse. Evil spreads like a virus, or like a wild fire—out of control. If a little evil is introduced into a group of people, soon the whole group will respond in an evil way. What is this seductive power of evil that overcomes us?

It was considered a major breakthrough for society when Hammurabi, 1792–1750 B.C., codified the laws of the Amorites, the original "eye for an eye and a tooth for a tooth." This law restrained human response so as not to escalate already tense situations. In previous times—to some extent even today—there are still cases where the seductive power of evil overflows and the retaliation is far worse than the initial offense. The escalation of aggression is often seen before countries go to all-out warfare, before a life or death fight develops between people, before a marriages are dissolved, before long-term friendships are broken. Hammurabi may have been able to control the civil laws of his land, but the hearts and minds of mankind have no such laws governing them. Evil waits at the door for an opportunity to enter and enrage the emotional responses for acts of even greater evil. What is this seductive power of evil?

The only clear explanation I have found is in the Bible, where the nature and power of Satan are described. Satan was the highest created being made by God. But he rebelled

195

against God and wanted to be higher than God. This battle between good and evil has been going on ever since, with Satan trying to subvert and destroy all God has created and loves. Satan and his fallen angels continuously bombard us with evil thoughts, feelings and temptations. How can we resist them? They come into our mind and bombard us. In many cases, they are stronger than the fear of the law or any forces others might bring against us. They are, in essence, self-destructive forces which, for the moment, are more important than any future consequences. This results in out of control action; our rational responses are bypassed. Our emotions overcome any restraint of reason and the results are disaster. This is the seductive power of evil.

What are we to do? Who is able to subdue and overcome Satan? Or, for that matter, know when he is influencing us, or when we are just responding with our human nature? Which is able to tell when are we being influenced by God and the Holy Spirit? We have three different natures, here, that should not be too hard to discern. God's nature is love, peace, joy, mercy, grace, holy and long suffering. He wants only the best for us. Satan's nature, on the other hand, is deception, lies, and temptations to do evil. He is intent on our destruction, death and keeping us separated from God. Our own human nature is self-serving, aggressive, pleasure-seeking, prideful, and demonstrates a lack of self-control. This state is an unstable condition between God and Satan; we can go either way. As we are without balance, our position in the middle will sway one way or the other. Unless God is on our side or, more correctly, we are on God's side, we have very little power to overcome Satan's influence and temptations to commit evil, and end up destroying ourselves in suffering and pain.

Jesus Christ said we are to respond with love, mercy and forgiveness, not return evil for evil. In the first paragraph of this essay, I am responding with evil for evil, not with love. Proverbs 15:1says, *"A gentle answer turns away wrath, but a harsh word stirs up anger"* and verse 18, *"A hot-tempered man stirs up dissension, but a patient man calms a quarrel"* So say many of the proverbs. The Hammaurbi Code only limits evil, it does not bring love and forgiveness. Yes, it takes more effort, energy and endurance to love someone who is unloving to us. Without the resources of the Holy Spirit within us, we could not prevail against the seductive power of evil. This is why Paul wrote, *"Put on the full armor of God so you can take your stand against the devil's schemes"* (Ephesians 6:11). Jesus commanded us to love one another as he loved us. That is an impossible task to do on our own, and difficult even with God's help.

WOUNDED BY SIN ················

I often struggle to find some analogy for the effects of sin. In our physical world the impact of sin is often neglected or, at most, considered an embarrassment. After all, everyone does it! We are just being natural; to sin is human. Many think that sin only has to do with those who believe and follow a particular religion, and that each religion has their own set of sins. If one does not believe or follow any religion, then there is no such thing as sin. This approach to thinking about sin does a great injustice to both the religious and the non-religious. Sin has a mortal impact on our being. How can this be? What is sin anyway?

Sin is not some arbitrary list of forbidden activities developed by a church committee long ago and forced on those who, for whatever reason, have chosen to follow that specific religion. Sin is a rebellion against the commandments given by the Creator of this universe. The determination, judgment and punishment for the transgression of these commandments are God's. As Christians it is not our responsibility to enforce God's commandments. We do have a responsibility to inform others of God's commandments and the penalty He gives to those who violate them.

God's punishment for the transgression of any of His commandments is death; eternal death. Not just physical death, which we all will experience, but a spiritual death. A separation from God and His kingdom, cast into a place of eternal torment called Hell. A place reserved for Satan and all his followers. God requires that we be perfect as He is perfect. Those are the standards we must meet to be chosen and adopted to be His children in Heaven. Sin results in a sentence of eternal Hell, Fire and Damnation. It is this aspect of sin from which we search for an escape.

The spiritual effects of sin can be compared to the physical effects of cancer. That dreaded word and herald of impending death! Our whole being goes into shock. There is very little we can do. The medical approach is very radical. Their attack on cancer is all out warfare; there are no means withheld in this battle; it may be radical surgery to remove major cancerous parts, or radiation treatment with deadly rays focused on known cancer areas to destroy the cells. It may be chemotherapy; poisoning of the body to kill the cancer and hope the rest will survive. These are serious life or death procedures. We should treat sin in such a manner.

Another physical example can be made by the bullet wounds our violent movies and TV bring us in such dramatic, vivid close-ups of the writhing pain shown in actors. I picture sin being like the bullets that produce such pain, suffering and death of our spiritual being. With bullets, the results are quick, dramatic and visible, unlike the silent and hidden works of sin on our bodies. The bullets' work is very visible, with lots of action, noise, blood and guts. With the same vigor we ban violence and guns, we should stop sinning.

We do not see the impact of sin upon our lives as readily as God does. He does not like to see His beautiful creation ruined by sin. Thus He banishes sinners from His kingdom; sin is a terminal condition. However, God has provided a way for the wounded sinners to return to health; there is a cure. God's Son, Jesus, paid the price through His death on the Cross taking all our sins with Him. God resurrected His Son, as He will do for us who have accepted Jesus Christ as our

Lord and Saviour. But we must recognize our wounded, sinful nature and sincerely ask Jesus to be healed of our sins.

Perhaps the hardest part is to recognize our sin wounds as we live in a society of wounded sinners; everyone is a walking, living sin-wounded person. Thus we must consider, is anyone perfect; that is without sin? Are we happy being imperfect like everyone else? One of the biggest unrecognized sins is pride; everyone has this to some degree. Are we willing to turn pride over to Jesus and accept His leadership? This may be harder then the more obvious sins that have recognizable physical impacts.

SIN MANAGEMENT ·················

It is quite obvious from the way people live that eliminating sin is impossible. The next best thing is Sin Management. This is like the old saying, "If you can't beat them, join them." Our culture has developed a major social system for Sin Management. We have government legislators with the help of lawyers passing "anti-sin" laws. Enforcement is executed by large, distributed groups of police officers. Then a court system administers the prosecution, judgment and sentencing. This is followed by a system of "correctional" facilities for those considered too seriously involved in sin to released back into society. It has long been hoped that our sin management system would reduce the seriousness and number of sinful events but, so far, progress is very slow.

Many complain that sin management has not significantly reduced the repeat offenders. That is, as one examines the sin management system, there are very little, if any, alternative lifestyle training or encouragement. Often, the jail approach is considered a sin school, where the inmates learn to sin and keep from being caught. After all, the sin management system is a big business and there are large profits and many jobs involved in this system. In fact, Americans have more people in jail per capita than any other nation. There are continual studies and evaluations to find new techniques for sin management.

Some people propose eliminating many activities from the "sin category" because of the total enforcement cost. It would be more economical for society just to let perpetrators do their thing. Others propose major educational and support programs to provide lifestyle changes to break the chain of repeat offenders; perhaps having public schools develop larger programs in sin prevention. A few are for increased penalties and more frequent use of the death penalty—just get rid of them. This would certainly reduce cost and solve some of the jail overcrowding. Isn't there a better way to manage sin?

Jesus Christ came to earth with a plan for Sin Control, not sin management. In the Old Testament there were elaborate procedures for Sin Management. God and his angels were the police, judge, jury, and jailer. When things got out of hand and people rebelled, it was out with the Flood, down with the Fire and Brimstone, walking to death in the desert, swallowed by earthquakes, and all sorts of plagues and other atrocities. God was very creative in His approach to punishment. But He also installed a pay-as-you-go sin system of sacrifices managed by the temple priests. If you conducted the self-punishment, you did not have to endure His imposed punishment. There were occasional problems with the priest system; after all they were only human. Still, this never achieved much in the way of changing lifestyles.

Jesus' New Deal was a major breakthrough in Sin Control. The way God figured it out, Jesus, His Son, would pay the price for all our sins. Such a deal! Also, to receive this offer of grace and pardon, one had to follow Jesus as Lord of their lives. Realizing the problems in changing one's lifestyle, God sent the Holy Spirit to dwell within us and to be our guide and enabler. It is still quite a struggle to follow Jesus with all the many temptations from Satan and his gang. However, there is a second phase to Jesus' New Deal. With the forgiveness on earth comes a free upgrade to eternal life in Heaven as one of God's Children. This must be put in perspective;

without the up-grade, one remains forever separated in the tourist class system whose destination is Hell with minimum facilities and amenities.

The New Deal is not a mandatory procedure. Everyone has the opportunity to evaluate and decide on their own. This New Deal does not violate the Bill of Rights in God's original Constitution, written before creation and published in the Holy Bible. The New Deal was unanimously approved by the Heavenly Triumvirate of God the Father, God the Son and God the Holy Spirit. The only opposition was from Satan and his representatives, but they had long blown their credibility, ethics, morals and any authority they may have had— besides, they had already been tried and sentenced as traitors of The Kingdom of Heaven.

It is not too late to accept Jesus' New Deal, but don't wait. it's for a limited time only; the offer is not good after death.

UNILATERAL FORGIVENESS OR BILATERAL NEGOTIATIONS ....

How do we settle differences with our friends? Other than maintaining hostilities or waiting for them to surrender, what can or should we do? There is really quite a dilemma. On one hand, Scripture says we are to forgive not just once, but many times. For me, to forgive does not really settle the problem. Each time I see or think about this person, I have to go through forgiveness all over again; the memory is still there and the pain comes back. It ends up being a constant struggle. Thus, I consider unilateral forgiveness not really the best solution. It is a solution when nothing better can be found.

The best solution is to talk to the person with whom you have difficulties, and try to resolve the differences. This requires a lot of effort and is often hard to accomplish. The main point is that whatever caused the splitting of ways cannot be undone. It is not possible in this world to go back and erase what happened even if we want to. In many cases, both sides consider they were right and justified in what they did. Thus, there may be no basis for negotiations. There are many layers to the problems in relationships between people. Consider the following cases:

Case 1: The two parties meet, discuss their differences and verbally agree to forgive each other with neither accepting the blame. They both go on their ways believing the other has forgiven them but, in actuality, the memories are still there and the relationship never does get back to the way it was before the unfortunate event. Why might this be? I believe it takes a sacrifice on one or both parties. By this, I don't mean paying the speeding ticket to the judge to settle your case with the local law. Legally, you are "forgiven," but it is still on your record and your insurance company may change its rates for your insurance. The impact of your sin is still with you.

Case 2: The two parties meet, discuss their difference and work out a settlement to which both parties agree. This holds better possibilities of reestablishing the relationship, but is still subject to problems. Consider the case of settling an insurance claim for your loss. You both come to an agreed price and that "settles" it. You have no further rights for compensation. This may result in a fair value and it may not. Future impacts of your loss may be uncovered later on, and there are no further negotiations without resorting to lawsuits or similar actions.

Case 3: The two parties meet, discuss their differences, and agree to continue working on their relationship, each one making sacrifices to keep the relationship going. For this to work, it must be a win-win solution, there must be sufficient value in the relationship to make the sacrifices voluntary. That is, each must receive value for their sacrifice. The relationship provides the missing elements each party has; the relationship is more valuable then the sum values of each person.

Now consider our relationship with God, which was "broken" before we even started. Does God unilaterally forgive or bilaterally negotiate? Some may say, "unilaterally forgive," but is that correct? After all God's Son, Jesus Christ, died for our transgressions before we did anything. However, we must accept His sacrifice, repent of our sins, and obediently follow Him. That, to me, seems more like bilateral negotiations.

Why do we accept God's offer of reconciliation? Why does God offer the possibility of reconciliation? It must be of great value to each party because the sacrifices are very significant.

What does it take for us to change our lifestyles? Many have been threatened by death from smoking, drinking, overeating and heart conditions, but have not changed their lifestyles. Somehow the sacrifice of their current lifestyle was not worth the continuation of life. So there really is a big sacrifice in changing our lifestyle; it is not a small, easy thing to do.

Next, why did God offer us reconciliation? He paid a major price, thus it must produce a major value to Him for restoring our relationship. Scripture states that God loves us unconditionally with a love that surpasses our under-standing—so great is His love for us whom He created. How can we refuse such an offer? Only by not understanding and appreciating the sacrifice that God has made and the love He has for us. The value of changing our lifestyle is salvation from eternal death and a loving relationship with God for-ever. We have far more to gain than lose by accepting His offer to negotiate.

WHAT IS GLORY? ················

First, we must consider a definition for "glory." According to Webster's Dictionary, glory is: 1a: praise, honor or distinction; b: worshipful praise, honor and thanksgiving; 2a: something that secures praise or renown; b: distinguished quality or asset; 3a: great beauty and splendor; b: the splendor and beatific happiness of Heaven; 4a: a state of great gratification or exaltation; b: a height of prosperity or achievement; and 5: ring or sport of light as in aureole or corona.

Next, we should consider the glory of people, places and things of this world and our universe. On the human side, there are the great athletes and sports players who excel in their performances. There are the academic and intellectual leaders of our society who have demonstrated superior knowledge and wisdom. There are the great politicians, company presidents and military leaders of the nations who achieve significant progress in society. There are also the celebrated spiritual leaders and their churches. Nature boasts a marvelous array of animals and plants. The animals reveal harmony in motion, coloration and dexterity. The plants show beautiful flowers, leaves and form. We have the mountains, valleys, rivers, beaches, and oceans. What spectacular vistas we have, from snow-capped peaks to the pounding surf along the shoreline, the vastness of the oceans from the stillness of the Doldrums to their dynamic tempest of hurricanes, water-spouts and tidal waves Overhead we have fleeting clouds, from puffy balls of cotton to dark, ominous, turbulent giants, and on to dense fog that obliterates both sight and sound. Farther away are the moon, sun and stars, the moon shining with its changing phases. We experience a magnificent canopy over our heads with breathtaking sunrises and sunsets, surprising meteor showers, the aurora and the green flash. We have the wonders of the stars, galaxies and nebula. All show forth the glory of creation in so many different ways. We are bewildered and amazed by all this glory!

However, if we give all this glory to the created which we can see, how much more glory we should give to the Creator whom we cannot see! Would it not be like removing the author from a book, song or art, or rejecting the manufacturer's name on our car or appliance, or even considering ourselves, our world and the cosmos as being a random, meaningless event in time and space without cause, purpose or source? The real glory is due to the Creator of all things. Then is it so difficult to give God the glory He deserves?

Consider our problem. How can we experience the glory of God, the Creator of all things and beings? It is not always something we directly see or encounter each day. Many times, it is a feeling, a consciousness, or awareness of something beyond ourselves. For the rare few, there has been a direct experience of God touching them, sometimes when in dire need, sometimes when in prayer and meditation, and sometimes when totally unexpected. As Scriptures point out, the more we talk to God and seek His will for our lives, the more He will be involved in our lives. As His children, He wants us to seek and ask Him about all that is on our hearts and minds. He will respond, generally in ways and times we do not expect. To see God's glory, we must be constantly alert and consciously looking for God's involvement in our lives. Then, we can give Him the glory He deserves and wants us to give Him. That is our purpose in life!

What is God's glory? It is the essence of describing God. It is what we observe in ourselves and the world around us that reveals the glory of God. It is from His glory that we are able to describe God. Thus, the glory of God describes not only who God is, but what He does—the outward manifestations of the eternal nature of God. Some may ask, "Why can't we see God and thus His glory? If we could see Him, we would not have all these problems of giving Him glory! Scripture states that if we looked into God's face, we would die—it would be too much for us, perhaps like looking at our sun at a very close distance. We would be instantaneously consumed and turned into a vapor. Scientists currently estimate our universe contains a thousand, billion, billion (10^{21}) suns, and God is certainly brighter! At that high energy level, not only would we be vapor, but even our atoms would be decomposed into subatomic particles, or even less. The key to looking at God is to have His radiating energy totally flow through us and not be absorbed. The way to this is left as an exercise for the student to work out while studying the Bible, for in Heaven we will be able to see God and His glory face-to-face.

GIVING GOD GLORY ··············

"Giving God Glory" sounds very good, but how do we do that? We don't see him, and, very seldom do we "talk" to Him, so how can we give God glory? It is very hard to give glory if God is not front and center in our lives, and if we do not see His work in our lives day-by-day. How can we see God's glory or, better yet, experience God's glory? If we could do this, then we would be more faithful, focused and frequent in giving God glory.

In reading the Scriptures, there are 296 passages declaring the glory of God: 166 in the Old Testament and 130 in the New Testament. Let us consider a few of them here:

"Holy, holy, holy is the Lord Almighty; the whole earth is filled with his glory" (Isaiah 6:3). Wherever we look and wherever we go, we can see God's glory.

"The heavens declare the glory of God; the skies proclaim the work of his hands" (Psalm 19:1). As we look up into the night sky, we see billions upon billions of stars, galaxies and nebula. The greater our technology, the better we can see God's glory.

> *My frame was not hidden from you when I was made in the secret place. When I was woven together in the depths of the earth, your eyes saw my unformed body. All the days ordained for me were written in your book before one of them came to be* (Psalm 139:15–16).

Just consider ourselves, from conception to birth to maturing, on to old age and then the passing into eternity. Our creation reveals the glory of God in each and every detail.

> *For God, who said, "Let light shine out of darkness," made his light shine in our hearts to give us the light of*

the knowledge of the glory of God in the face of Christ (2 Corinthians 4:6). It is through knowing Jesus Christ that we see the full glory of God as it is revealed on earth.

"So whether you eat or drink or whatever you do, do it all for the glory of God" (1 Corinthians 10:31). All things should remind us of the glory of God.

And we know that in all things God works for the good of those who love him, who have been called according to his purpose (Romans 8:28).

I consider that our present sufferings are not worth comparing with the glory that will be revealed in us. The creation waits in eager expectation for the sons of God to be revealed. For the creation was subjected to frustration, not by its own choice, but by the will of the one who subjected it, in hope that the creation itself will be liberated from its bondage to decay and brought into the glorious freedom of the children of God (Romans 8:18–21).

Jesus said, *"In this world you will have trouble. But take heart! I have overcome the world"* (John 16:33). We do not fully understand the glory God has prepared for us when we get to Heaven.

I have become its servant by the commission God gave me to present to you the work of God in its fullness—the mystery that has been kept hidden for ages and generations, but is now disclosed to the saints. To them God has chosen to make known among the Gentiles the glorious riches of this mystery, which is Christ in you, the hope of glory (Colossians 1:27).

Paul's words remind us that life on earth is a mystery; a glorious mystery.

All men are like grass, and all their glory is like the flowers of the field; the grass withers and the flowers fall, but the word of the Lord stands forever (1 Peter 1:24).

Our glory is shortlived, but the glory of God continues throughout all eternity.

Then I saw another angel flying in midair, and he had the eternal gospel to proclaim to those who lived on earth—to every nation, tribe, language and people. He said in a loud voice, 'Fear God and give him glory, because the hour of his judgment has come. Worship him who made the heavens, the earth, the sea and the springs of water (Revelation 14:6–7).

John's vision prepares us for the Judgement Day. As we give God glory, we put ourselves in proper relationship to God. We can only do that as we understand how little we have accomplished that has eternal value. All that we have done and accumulated on earth will pass away.

The great story of life is the battle between good and evil in which we have been enmeshed between two great forces. God created the cosmos and all that is within it and called it "Good." It was a glorious world. Then Satan attacked, leading a great rebellion against God, taking us down with him. Now God has come to our rescue through His Son, Jesus Christ, who paid with His perfect life to ransom us from the Forces of Darkness by paying our sin debt and releasing us to become Children of God. For the true Kingdom, the Power and the Glory are His, forever and ever.

THE GLORY OF GOD ON DISPLAY ∙∙∙∙∙∙∙∙∙∙∙∙∙∙∙

What do you mean, "The Glory of God on Display"? We don't see God's glory anywhere around here! The best we have here is, "The Glory of Man on Display." Well, maybe if we go off to the mountains, the deserts, the coast-line or the oceans we may see "The Glory of Nature on Display." But that does not look anything we would expect to see! Personally, I see problems, clutter, confusion, disharmony, pollution, and the need for maintenance than any glory. So where do we go to see the glory of God on display?

To begin, what do the Scriptures say about the glory of God on display? Perhaps this will give us some ideas where to look. Consider the Psalms:

"O Lord, our Lord, how majestic is your name in all the earth! You have set your glory above the heavens" (8:1).

"The heavens declare the glory of God; the skies proclaim the work of his hands" (19:1).

"In the heavens he has pitched a tent for the sun" (19:4).

"I love the house where you live, O Lord, the place where your glory dwells" (26:8).

"By the word of the Lord were the heavens made, their starry host by the breath of his mouth" (33:6).

"Be exalted, O God, above the heavens, and let your glory be over all the earth" (108:5).

"The Lord is exalted over all the nations, he glory above the heavens" (113:4).

In other sections of the Bible we have:

God came from Teman, the Holy One from Mount Param. His glory covered the heavens and his praise filled the earth (Habakkuk 3:3).

"But Stephen, full of the Holy Spirit, looked up to heaven and saw the glory of God" (Acts 7:55).

"Heaven is my throne, and the earth is my footstool" (Acts 7:49).

There are also heavenly bodies and there are earthly bodies; but the splendor of the heavenly bodies is one kind, and the splendor of the earthly bodies is another. The sun has one kind of splendor, the moon another and the stars another; and star differs from star in splendor (1 Corinthians 15:40–41).

Consider further:

For you created my inmost being; you knit me together in my mother's womb. I praise you because I am fearfully and wonderfully make; your works are wonderful, I know that full well (Psalm 139:14).

Then there is a warning:

The wrath of God is being revealed from heaven against all the godlessness and wickedness of men who suppress the truth by the wickedness, since what may be know about God is plain to them, because God has made it plain to then. For since the creation of the world God's invisible qualities—his eternal power and divine nature—have been clearly seen, being understood from what has been made, so that men are without excuse (Romans 1:18–20).

But do we declare the glory of God? The first problem we encounter is being able to recognize the glory of God when we see it. If we do not see God's handiwork around us, how can we give Him glory? It is very, very seldom that anyone directly sees the bright radiance that surrounds God; just a few instances have been recorded in the Bible. Adam and Eve talked to God in the cool of the day (Genesis 3:8); Moses on Mt. Sinai received the law and instructions from God in Exodus 19. Isaiah saw the Lord high and lifted up (Isaiah 6:1). Jesus' disciples Peter, James and John were present at the transfiguration on the mountain, given in Matthew 17. Finally, John on the island of Patmos is taken up in the spirit to see Jesus Christ in Heaven (Revelation 1).

For the rest of us, His glory is reflected in His handiwork, seen in the stars, galaxies, nebula and planets which surrounds us in the heavens. The glory of God can be in the beauty of a sunrise or sunset, in the oceans, beaches, valleys and mountains around us, even in all the living beings, shown by the miracle of birth. It is demonstrated by the love that shines through those around us who reflect the love of Jesus Christ. To see the glory of God all around requires spiritual recognition. For what glory is there in us and the things we have made? We may paint them, or illuminate them, or elevate them, but it is all a false glory, the false glory of our fallen nature. Unfortunately, we are not immune from seeking and being given the world's glory. The more recognition we receive and the higher our position in society, the harder it is for God's glory to shine. Let us always keep in balance the glory of being created by God, being his children, living in this world, and God's glory shining through us to show the world the true light of truth. Our worldly glory will quickly fade and become nothing, but the glory of God is eternal and ever-present. Give God the praise He deserves.

RADIATING, REFLECTING OR ABSORBING GLORY ·················

I enjoy turning my telescope to the heavens and observing the glory of the universe created by God. There are two types of light I observe—one is the direct radiation from stars that use various nuclear and atomic processes to generating a wide-spectrum light. The other is the reflected light by the planets, moons, asteroids, and nebula from nearby stars. Their emissions are passive; they do not generate the light we observe. Without their reflected light, it is doubtful we would ever see them except as they pass in front of an illuminating source. In addition, dust clouds leave dark, irregular patches and blot out major regions of our own Milky Way Galaxy. Our summer night skies would be even more brilliant if it were not for these obscuring clouds of early formation debris. The absorption of light, in this case, reduces the glory of the heavens we see.

Without the sun both illuminating the earth and providing the energy for heat so that life can survive, plants can grow and produce food, water can evaporate to create the clouds that water the land, our earth would just be another big cold rock floating in space. With that very constant energy flow, which is reflected, transmitted and absorbed, and the protective filter layer of atmosphere, the sun produces an environment of incredible beauty and all the resources needed for life. The sun provides the radiating energy which is reflected, transmitted and absorbed in the various layers and substances. So, do we give all the glory to the sun? No, the sun's energy is absorbed and converted to many other manifestations of this energy. The glory is in this transforming process of the sun's energy and all the life and change produced.

What about human glory? I have my list of those who have demonstrated outstanding abilities and deserve recognition and glory. The media has their own list, which I believe is influenced by the ratings and rewards they receive. Every organization I know has their special list of members who receive glory. It is a natural process in our society to give out glory awards. We think of the movie Oscars, the sports Hall of Fame, Olympics Gold Medals, the academic and social contributions with the Nobel Prizes, the soldiers' Medals of Valor, to name a few. Everyone appreciates being recognized for their hard work and achievements. I even have a few plaques on the wall, one being for Engineer of the Year from the Lockheed Corporation—my glory award. But are these really our achievements and our glory?

Much of what we accomplish in life has to do with what we started with in natural abilities, talents and family resources. Some just have more than others, and they did not have anything to do with that. However, when it comes to putting our abilities and talents into action, and perfecting our profession, that is where we begin to have some control. We may or may not develop our potential. There is need for motivation and encouragement. The discipline to become a top competitor in any field takes a lot of work, perseverance, focus and sacrifice. We cannot do everything well. We must pick and choose what we do. To whom do we listen for advice and counsel? How do we make our decisions?

Our family, friends and teachers have a big role in guiding our future. In many cases, one must start early to become a top achiever in a field. This requires more guidance from our mentors than our own decisions, but our responsiveness and commitment are very important. In some cases, God steps in and gives a calling, such as going into the ministry. For what God calls us to do, He also provides all that is needed for us to meet His call. However, how do we know He has not been working behind the scenes all the time in everyone's life? After all, Scripture notes that God had a plan and purpose for our lives ordained before the beginning of creation. The only difference is that some have followed God's plan and some have followed their own plan. For those who followed God's plan, obviously, God should get the glory. For those who followed their own plan, they deserve what they get (most likely second or third best). God's plan for our lives is to receive our glory in Heaven for a job well done on earth. So how are we doing; are we just absorbing, actively reflecting or transforming and radiating God's glory?

ABSORBING AND APPLYING THE GLORY ········

I had great dreams and ambitions when I went off to college. I had a vision of knowledge and wisdom piled higher and deeper (Ph.D), and all the professors who were going to teach me. All I had to do was absorb all they said, read all the text books and that would be it. Well, maybe a test or two, some lab work and a few term papers. So I worked hard, studied hard, memorized hard, did all the assignments and took the tests. I graduated with a few glory degrees of education in the sciences, certified by the professors, and went off to work to do great things for society. I had absorbed the knowledge and wisdom.

I started work with great enthusiasm; I was now ready to apply my glory. I was going to be able to use all that stored knowledge and wisdom I had worked so hard to accumulate. My first assignment? Go to the workbench and test, calibrate and repair equipment that was built by others. Not quite the big dreams I had. There was a big gap between head knowledge and hand knowledge—from absorption to application. I had to figure out how to use all that stored education. There was very little training and education about the real, mundane and practical aspects of using all that knowledge and wisdom. I had a lot to learn about the practical working world. The world we live in is not as "perfect" as the laws, theories and computer models we use all the time in design and analysis. I had absorbed a lot of facts and figures along with the glory of higher education from a top university in science, but now I had to make it all work!

There was another factor I was not fully prepared for, my "glory" title. I started as a junior engineer-scientist. That meant I got to do what no one else wanted to do. In the beginning, I had very little selection in job assignments. However, I did have the privilege of working with some of the top scientists, and learned much from them. It was like school all over again, but at least I got paid for it. We conducting research on the effects of meteors, the aurora and nuclear weapons on communications and radar performance. I ended up calibrating, running and maintaining the equipment while the senior scientists took the data and did the analysis. At least my name ended up on the research report, even if it was at the end of the list. Slowly, but surely, I was promoted up the "glory" ladder with bigger titles, larger salaries and more responsibilities.

There is another "school" I have been attending; this is the spiritual school of life run by Jesus Christ. I began as an Inquirer, trying to figure out what the world and life were all about. This included both the theory as well as the field work. I studied hard and did my homework through the years—the absorbing part of the operation. I progressed to Candidate. This involved understanding the requirements for advancement into membership and being more active in our local church group. I took many classes on the Bible and even a few on how to teach the Bible. I enjoyed sitting in class learning about the deeper truths of Scripture. Eventually, I came to the point of commitment and was promoted into Membership in the Family of God—I could now apply God's Word. In the beginning, I thought I had done it all and was ready for anything. In fact, I was just beginning as an Apprentice!

It is not obvious that I will ever graduate from apprenticeship. I still have difficulty following all the Boss's rules and commandments. As well, the Boss does not grow old, slow down and retire. It is a good thing too, because as hard as I may try, I will never catch up with the Him in knowledge, wisdom and power. Is it so bad to be an apprentice and never have a future of one day being in charge of everything? If we have a very good boss who gives us assignments that are better than what we would chosen by ourselves, then an eternal relationship as an apprentice is a good as it gets.

Yes, the big Boss does talk about a promotion, from work on earth to work in Heaven as His faithful apprentice. The old tools we had with our mortal body will be replaced with new abilities in our immortal body. All the old aches, pains, suffering and death will be gone forever. We will be able to talk to the Boss face-to-face, not as it is now with vague generalities and messages passed along by written Words and inspired comments from others. There is no end to absorbing and applying God's glory.

PANNING FOR GLORY ···············

Clarence was up on 40 Mile, tributary to the great Yukon River, panning and getting very little pay dirt in the summer of 1896. He was looking for the big glory hole. Was it just around the bend in the stream? Perhaps. Maybe on another stream all together different! Clarence was a heavy-set, muscular man, having worked the farms in Central California. After going bankrupt twice farming, it was time to try something else to obtain fortune and glory. He was determined to strike it rich in the Yukon. If farming had not brought the glory, maybe gold panning would. After all, there was a beautiful young lady back home he was very interested in.

In Bill McFee's saloon late that afternoon, Clarence was considering his meager findings and thinking there had to be a better way. A man came in the bar and put down a big poke of gold dust and said, "Drinks for the house!" Immediately the whole room came alive, awakened from long months of just barely surviving on their findings. "What was this?" "Where did all that gold come from?" The excitement raised to a high pitch and all eyes and ears were on this stranger. His name was George Carmack and he had found the big glory river, Bonanza Creek, with course gold dust and nuggets in great abundance. "Let's all celebrate!"

Well, Clarence's celebration was out the back door; he grabbed all his stuff, and poled up the 40 Mile to Dawson as fast as he could go. This was a once-in-a-lifetime opportunity and it was not going to be missed! Yes, it was poling through the night up the big river, but there was a bit of the moon to help. Besides, there was no time to waste! Everyone else would soon be on the trail.

He was right about everyone else coming. This was the beginning of the largest gold rush in history! Men came from all around the world, but Clarence had a one-year headstart on almost all of them! The rest is history, with his name recorded in almost every record and book on the Great Klondike Stampede. He found his glory and provided a legacy for the future!

Most of those who found their glory in gold never found their glory in life. Many died young and penniless. Just a few ever made it out of the Klondike with their great wealth, and very few of those had anything left to pass along to the next generation. Others became disillusioned over the great rigors of the quest and turned back or died in the process. The trails were long and steep, the rivers wild and treacherous, and everything had to be transported into this wilderness land. Each man had to bring 2,000 pounds of goods before the Canadian Mounties would allow them to enter the Yukon. There were few provisions along the trail and the prices were astronomical.

There are great riches in the gold of this world, but where is the great value in life? Isn't life more precious than gold or silver? How many pan through the world's treasures looking for the glory of life and never find it? For narrow is the path and confining are the ways that lead to the glory of life—glories of love, joy, peace, patience, kindness, goodness, faithfulness, gentleness and self-control, all described as the fruits of the Spirit in the Scriptures. They are not found by panning through what the world values, but through what God values; these things lie partially hidden all around us. We have to go panning for God's glory to find its great rewards. For God is the source of all the glory of life; not just life on this planet, but life for all eternal.

How can we go through life searching the whole earth, and not find the treasures of life? Perhaps this has to do with the "treasures" we are looking for. Do we seek power, honor, recognition, wealth, influence, and security for ourselves? These are temporal and can come and go at the whim of time. There are but a few years to life in this world and then, all is gone like a vapor. It is like striving against the wind. Solomon said, "All is vanity" (Ecclesiastes 1:2 KJV) in describing much of his life in Ecclesiastes. The true treasures of life are found by panning the Word of God in the Bible, and putting them into practice in our lives. These are eternal treasures and bring life in abundance both for now and into eternity. It is through fulfilling God's Word that we become Children of God and inherit all the riches and glory of Heaven. The true spiritual gold is worth the panning.

TRANSFORMING INANIMATENESS ···············

What would it take for us to become like a dead man, that is, prostrate and motionless? It would take an emotional shock of the greatest magnitude. A physical force that overwhelms us, an energy field that neutralizes our total neural system. What could possibly cause this inanimateness? Is this even possible?

We have seen football games where a player had the wind knocked out of him and down he went. I once hit my big toe with a sledgehammer when splitting wood. The pain brought me to the ground. Also, I used to work for the San Diego Gas and Electric company on a line crew. There were many stories about high voltage rendering the neural system inoperative; the affected became as dead men. If something was not done quickly, they soon would be dead men!

There is more to all this, however, than we have so far covered; consider our spiritual dynamics.

In the Bible we have many stories about encounters with angels, and even God:

> On the morning of the third day there was thunder and lightning, with a thick cloud over the mountain, and a very loud trumpet blast. Everyone in the camp trembled. ... Mount Sinai was covered with smoke, because the Lord descended on it in fire. The smoke billowed up from it like smoke from a furnace, the whole mountain trembled violently, and the sound of the trumpet grew louder and louder. Then Moses spoke and the voice of God answered him (Exodus 19:16–19).

I think that would be enough to stop anyone dead in their tracks. Read the example of Zechariah:

Then an angel of the Lord appeared to him, standing at the right side of the alter of incense. When Zechariah saw him, he was startled and was gripped with fear. But the angel said to him: "Do not be afraid"... (Luke 1:11–13).

Why did the angel have to say, "Do not be afraid?" Because Zechariah was acting like a dead man. Another example:

And there were shepherds living out in the field nearby, keeping watch over their flocks at night. An angel of the Lord appeared to them, and the glory of the Lord shone around them, and they were terrified. But the angel said to them, "Do not be afraid" (Luke 2:8–10). They were scared to death!

Saul had the same reaction when he was on his way to Damascus to persecute disciples of Jesus:

Suddenly a light from heaven flashed around him. He fell to the ground and heard a voice say to him, "Saul, Saul, why do you persecute me?" "Who are you, Lord?" Saul asked. "I am Jesus, whom you are persecuting," he replied (Acts 9:3–5).

The spiritual light from Heaven rendered him powerless and sightless. What else could he do?

We have no personal experience of the glory of God in all His holiness, power and magnificence. All we have seen are distorted (corrupted by the darkness of sin), reflected images of God's glory in this world and the universe around us. The full view of Heaven and all its dimensions would transform us into inanimateness. Consider Isaiah's experience:

227

I saw the Lord seated on a throne, high and exalted, and the train of his robe filled the temple. Above him were seraphs… "Woe to me!" I cried. "I am ruined! For I am a man of unclean lips, and I live among a people of unclean lips, and my eyes have seen the King, the Lord Almighty" (Isaiah 6:1–2,5).

Isaiah was convinced he was going to die. Such a sight was far too wonderful for a human to endure. John relates the same type of experience in Revelation:

On the Lord's Day I was in the Spirit, and I heard behind me a loud voice like a trumpet… .I turned around to see the voice that was speaking to me. And when I turned I saw seven golden lampstands, and among the lampstands was someone "like a son of man," dressed in a robe reaching down to his feet and with a golden sash around his chest. His head and hair were white like wool, as white as snow, and his eye were like blazing fire. His feet were like bronze glowing in a furnace, and his voice was like the sound of rushing waters. In his right hand he held seven stars, and out of his mouth came a sharp double-edge sword. His face was like the sun shining in all its brilliance. When I saw him, I fell at his feet as though dead. Then he placed his right hand on me and said: "Do not be afraid. I am the First and the Last. I am the Living One: I was dead, and behold I am alive for every and ever! And I hold the keys of death and Hades" (Revelation 1:10,12–20).

Are we ready to meet the Lord? It is not too late to prepare!

WHAT DID GOD DO THE SECOND WEEK? ......

The Book of Genesis outlines God's activities in creation over the first seven days. In light of this observation, the natural question is "What did God do the second week?" The debate still rages. There are no specific and definitive answers given in the Scriptures, thus we are left to our own speculations, theories and logic. How could anything be greater than the first week of creation? After all, we do not expect God to be about doing the casual, the insignificant and the meaningless! He has left that for us to do. Genesis states that we are to be productive, to manage and care for His creation.

What would be parallel to God's act of creation? It should be something great, challenging and unexpected, but in the same nature and in character as God demonstrated the first week. How shall we approach this? First, consider the revelations of Scripture in Genesis, after creation. Satan comes along and does his best to mess it all up and take charge. I see this as part of The Great Cosmic Chess Game; Satan moves and God counters, Satan challenges and God blocks, Satan claims "Check" and God moves to "Checkmate." Thus, from this point of view, God's second week is the chess game with Satan. From Genesis 3 through to most of Revelation is a blow-by-blow description of the battle between God and Satan. The challenge of titans, though in reality, Satan is no match for God. The endgame was known before the challenge began.

Oh, yes, there are a few side games in progress during this second week. One is God sending His Son, Jesus Christ, to earth to rescue those who are on God's side, trapped on the battlefield where He and Satan are in confrontation and claiming victory over the human souls they have captured. Throughout this entire engagement, God has provided a shield for those who have been chosen to be on His side. Satan cannot attack God's Elect without getting permission from God first. Furthermore, God uses Satan's attacks for His purpose to further refine and perfect His chosen children. Satan always ends up in a "lose-lose" situation. Nevertheless, he continues to add to his collection of souls from the human population. He is amassing a great army in preparation for the final battle. Before this great and terrible battle takes place, Jesus Christ will return and gather all God's children who have given their allegiance to Him, Lord of Lords and King of Kings. The Great Tribulation and War will follow. What a wonderful day of victory this will be for God and His followers.

Has God been busy in His second week? Yes indeed, very busy. He personally listens and cares for each of His chosen children day-by-day, moment-by-moment. With His mighty right hand He has countered every blow from Satan and rendered Satan harmless against His children. However, the battle is drawing to a close and the end is soon. Then what?

It will then be the Third Week! At the end of Revelation we read of the New Heaven and the New Earth. All things will be new; there will be no more pain, no more suffering and no more death. There will be a great banquet where all God's children are welcomed into His Kingdom in Heaven. Such a glorious time it will be. Satan, his demons and all those following him will have been cast into the remotest of places called Hell, and there be separated for all eternity from God and His children. Finally there will be peace, joy and love in the New World.

SECOND GENESIS? ••••••••••••••

We are quite familiar with the First Genesis, that in six days (or periods of time) God created the universe, our world and all living beings, and on the seventh day He rested.

But what is this Second Genesis? Do we believe that God is still in His seventh day of rest? Would not a creative God who made the universe, the world and all living beings get an itch to do some more creational works, even bigger and better? Certainly we are not at the peak of everything being perfect. Is going back to the Garden of Eden in a restored condition as good as it gets? I believe in a God who is more creative than that. Many do not!

Remember the Jews who had been freed from Egyptian bondage by God's miracles, and promised a land flowing with milk and honey? They spent forty years wandering through the desert and thinking of how nice is was back in Egypt. They would not have wandered so long if they had just accepted God's promise of a land flowing with milk and honey, and gone to possess the land. Most of them could only think about going back to the old ways of their past.

Consider where we are today. Jesus came about 2,000 years ago and set us free from the bondage of our sins. We are no longer captives of our sins and condemned to death. We are free. Yet for the last 2,000 years we have been wandering this world—our desert experience—complaining about all the things that are going wrong. We think about Jesus coming back, restoring our world and being in charge as our King, a King with truth, mercy and justice. Scriptures do point to the second coming of Jesus. I believe many of us, including myself, think of how nice we had it when we were children and our parents took care of all our needs; we want to go back to the way thing were. Which would we choose, back to our childhood, or onward to Heaven? The known or the unknown? God has something much better for us!

What do the Scriptures say about the Second Genesis? Consider Jesus' comments in John 14:1–4:

> Do not let your hearts be troubled. Trust in God, trust also in me. In my Father's house are many rooms; if it were not so, I would have told you. I am going there to prepare a place for you. And if I go and prepare a place for you, I will come back and take you to be with me that you also may be where I am.

That sounds like some creational work to me, and not in the Garden of Eden, but in Heaven. There is more: John writes in Revelation 21:1–4:

> Then I saw a new heaven and a new earth, for the first heaven and the first earth had passed away, and there was no longer any sea. I saw the Holy City, the new Jerusalem, coming down out of heaven from God, prepared as a bride beautifully dressed for her husband. And I heard a loud voice from the throne saying, 'Now the dwelling of God is with men, and he will live with them. They will be his people, and God himself will be with them and be their God. He will wipe every tear from their eyes. There will be no more death or mourning or crying or pain, for the old order of things has passed away.

More discussion of the New Jerusalem follows—a cube, 1,400 miles on a side! This sounds far better than the restored Eden or earth. Who would want to return to the old earth or

Eden, given the promise of the glories of a new creation and living with God for eternity?

Many cults and other religions have their own version of life-after-death, a dreamworld of man's imagination. Yet we are so limited; our dreamworld would be nothing like God's perfect creations. In this context, our dreamworld would be like Hell compared to God's creation and His design for the Second Genesis.

It is only by faith that we can enter into God's new creation. All others will be separated to a place, perhaps like that of their dreams though, in reality, Hell. Consider being on a small, isolated island in the Pacific Ocean. Very, very soon, we would get tired of the limited variations, the unchanging seasons, the same thing to eat and drink year after year. There would be nothing significant to do. That would indeed be like Hell after the first hundred or thousand years.

Therefore, keep the faith and praise the Lord, for He has promised an eternity with us in the new Genesis. Who knows, perhaps there is a third, fourth, or maybe even more Geneses.

THE UNCOMMON LOGIC OF CHRISTIANITY ···

First, what is "logic"? The word is from the Greek and, basically defined, means, "the science of the formal principles of knowledge." Second, what is "uncommon"? It is often defined as, "not ordinarily encountered." Thus, we are concerned about "The science of the formal principles of knowledge not ordinarily encountered." How, we may ask, can this apply to Christianity? Are not most religions a practice of faith, not logic? How can Christianity be different? It claims God has given us the absolute truth, knowledge and wisdom to sets us free from error. Therefore, it is subject to rules of logic, testing and verification. We are challenged by Christianity in its uncommon logic to carefully evaluate its truth, knowledge and wisdom. How do we do this?

First, let us see what is said about God in the Bible and compare that to what we see in our world. Genesis states that God created the heavens, the earth and all living beings. Now, those are physical things we can use our natural logic to examine. In fact, we have created advanced sciences for each of these areas, using logic, knowledge and wisdom to develop our data.

Since God's creations should reveal His nature, what does science tell us about God? We discover that God is very organized, structured, complex, continuous over very long spans of time and space, with great flare for detail both in the very small and the very large. Everything operates in a very delicate balance and is integrated in a beautiful way. There is an incredible amount of information we have gathered and put into our laws, theories and observations. We are far from knowing how everything works, how it all began and how it will all end. However, what we do have is a system that is very stable, repeatable, continuous and universal. In many ways our lives are dependent upon the nature of this universe. Thus, these characteristics of creation should be the very same characteristics revealed of God in the Bible. If not, it would stand to reason that God was not its creator.

Further in Genesis, we read that God created mankind in His image. We are not gods, but we have the general characteristics of God. That is, we are children of God. We have many of the aspects of God, but not His full knowledge, power and wisdom. Unfortunately, the many aspects of God are not what we observe in most people. What we find is selfishness, greed, lust, anger, violence and war. Something is wrong with our model.

What does the Bible say about this? We find a major gap between us and God. It is as though we have metamorphosed from God's children into something else. How can this be? Scriptures comment that Satan came and tempted man and woman to defy God and consume the forbidden fruit of the knowledge of good and evil. But when man and woman did, they found they could not handle this knowledge and it ended in their death—separation from God in spiritual death and, eventually, separation from the world in physical death. At this point, we must consider ourselves alienated from God, not having His characteristics and not His true children. The Scriptures describe us as children of Satan because we follow his ways of deception, deceit, and destruction. One might naturally ask, "What do we have to do with God and what does He have to do with us?" Is it not as though God might as well not exist?

Yes, but God's love is so great that He sent His only Son, Jesus, to earth to show us how we should live, to become a sacrifice for our sins against God, through the crucifixion. God then revealed His great power of salvation through res-urrection of His dead Son, a demonstration of His promise of what He will do for us if we follow His Son as our Lord and Master. It is our way to return to the indwelling of His nature and again become children of God. This explains the gap between our present loss of God's nature and the promise of future restoration for everything renew—a new Heaven, a new Earth and a new Jerusalem.

We are challenged by all the sciences and throughout all the pages of Scripture to find this uncommon logic that ties the Christian God to the world we know. It is a long and rig-orous path, but worthy of those who pursue it, for the rewards, the peace and the joys are great. Furthermore, if our faith is not based on logic, of what value is our faith? Without true faith, it is impossible to have a relationship with God. Without a relationship with God, it is impossible to know true love. Without God's love, it is impossible to love His cre-ation, not to mention accept Jesus Christ as our Lord and Saviour, thereby inheriting our rightful place as Children of God for all eternity in Heaven with Him. This is truly a most uncommon logic.

FORTY YEARS IN THE DESERT AND GOING NOWHERE ·················

When I read Exodus, the part where the Jews are wandering forty years in the desert and going nowhere, I think of how frustrating this must have been. Imagine spending forty years of your life, not accomplishing anything, just surviving. What a severe punishment this was! Very few of our present crimes result in a forty-year imprisonment without parole. Now, God did not have a physical prison, but wandering around aimlessly in the desert would seem to me like a prison sentence. In fact, it was worse than that. God sentenced the people twenty years and older, to a lifeterm. They were going to wander around in the desert until they all died off. All of this for not believing God and His offer of the Promised Land flowing with "milk and honey."

Consider, it is really any different today? Where are we going with our lives? We may work forty years of our lives and what have we accomplished? Just a retirement plan? Just a collection of materialistic possessions? Just a collection of experiences? To what purpose? Death is the next stop after retirement. Can we really say this is any different than wandering forty years in the desert? Isn't our sentence of death the same as those of the Jews in the wilderness? We have not found the Promised Land, but the gospel is God's invitation to do so. Retirement may be better than working 8-5, but I would not consider it a land flowing with milk and honey—even if those items were on my diet. What are we missing?

God promised those who love and follow Him the "Promised Land," both on earth and in Heaven. We already know the Heaven part. Jesus said,

In my Father's house are many rooms; if it were not so, I would have told you. I am going there to prepare a place for you... I will come back and take you to be with me that you also may be where I am (John 14:2,3).

In Heaven we will live with Him forever; no more pain, no more suffering and no more death. Yet what about on earth? Here we can receive the fruits (the milk and honey) of the Spirit; love, joy, peace, patience, kindness, goodness, faithfulness, gentleness and self-control (Galatians 5:22–23). What would we think of a land that give us all these fruits? Would it not be like the "Promised Land?" On the other hand, I do not find the promises of no suffering, pain and death on earth. This was not promised Moses and Abraham, nor was it promised those who follow Jesus Christ. Jesus said,

If they persecuted me, they will persecute you also... In this world you will have trouble. But take heart! I have overcome the the world (John 15:20,33).

This is Satan's world, what more could we expect for those who love God? Satan is not about to make our lives enjoyable. Be concerned if we are not being persecuted! We may be deceived by Satan and follow him, wandering aimlessly through this world. Jesus has given us work to do before we leave for Heaven. We are not without purpose on this fallen earth; we must bring the message of hope and salvation to those who are lost and trapped. We continue to exist on earth because of God's protection. Without that, Satan would have eliminated us long ago.

Our forty or more years of life on earth (our desert) have meaning even if we must go through persecution. They will strengthen our faith in God and illuminate His great power and love. These years allow us to see our weaknesses and learn to depend upon Him. The continuing revelations of God more than offset the trouble we have on earth. Additionally, in Heaven all our sufferings and death will be insignificant, compared to the glory of being with Jesus.

Is our earth really so different than a desert? There is a great spiritual death over the earth, just like the physical lack of life in the desert. A desert is not a friendly environment. The heat, cold, dryness, and loneliness in the void of life brings a harshness to living. It is just as the spiritual death on our earth creates emptiness, and the loss of significance and meaning in our lives. It is important to share Jesus' message of God's love and salvation with those around us who do not realize the full potential of life—spiritual life on earth and eternal life in Heaven. We do not *have* to live in a desert on earth or be condemned to the eternal separation reserved for Satan and his followers.

MAGNIFYING THE SCRIPTURES ················

As I read through the Bible I rapidly come to the conclusion that everything has been significantly compressed and a lot of very important data has been lost. It is like someone put the full, unabridged story through a magic concentrator that extracted only the bare essentials. Only in very few places are there any duplications or cross references. The most notable exceptions are within the four Gospels of Jesus Christ's time on earth; each writer gives a slightly different viewpoint. This is one of the major highlights of the whole Book. Why is it that the Bible seems so condensed? What should we do about it? How can we magnify Scripture?

First off, where does all this compression come from? This results from the many dimensions of our natural being. The written word is essentially one-dimensional; it goes in one direction and has no conditions on time—we can read as slow or as fast as we want. The spoken word has two dimensions; time is now added. Also, a picture has two dimensions—height and width but no depth or time. The time can be added with movies, video or the like. There is still no dimension of depth—that takes a 3-D projection either in still pictures or movies.

We are not yet at the full expanse of our five senses: sight, sound, smell, taste, feel, and some add the 6th sense of intuition and insight. When we experience life, we "see" it in all its natural dimensions. Our universe has more dimensions then we realize. All dimensions must be present to achieve the full magnification of life's experiences.

The second phase of compression comes in two forms. The most obvious is the information lost in translation. The surrounding culture, customs and events of the people are not given in detail, but these things would have been obvious if we were there at that time. Only the major events are given, with the focus on a few of the main characters; most of the background information is lost. Many years are often skipped over, in and between the books, chapters and verses.

The last point is that we seldom know what God is doing and thinking. It is only through the prophets and major judgements that God's views are revealed—yes, Jesus does tell us about the Father, but we seldom know for sure what transpired between Him and His Father during prayers.

Historians, archeologists, geologists, sociologists, linguists and many other specialists who research the past have provided, and continue to add to, the background chronological information about the culture, customs and events that occurred during Biblical times. From this information we can develop a general idea of what the people, places and things were like.

The account of creation has been a special concern and area of study for the scientists and cosmologists. Many of these "experts" have conflicting views of what happened. We have occasionally visited historical sites such as Colonial Williamsburg to ask those portraying characters of the early times, along with historical experts, what the real conditions were like. There are a number of conditions they do not include or simulate such as the very smokey, dim, candlelit rooms, the body odor of those who infrequently bathed themselves or washed their clothes, having no screens on windows, and the piles of horse manure and mud in the streets, along with the minimum sanitary facilities.

We have many translations and paraphrases of the Scriptures; each believe theirs is better presentation of the real story. In many cases, there are ambiguities in the meanings of the original text. Thus, there is no agreement in the translations, interpretations and the commentaries on the meaning of the text. How are we ever going to get back to the unabridged story? How can we magnify the Scriptures so we understand the full story?

There is only one source we can turn to as all the original characters and writers are dead—except Jesus, but He is now at the right had of the Father in Heaven. Who might that source be? The one and only Holy Spirit! One of His roles in our lives is to explain and give us an understanding of the Scriptures. His can fill in all the details; He was there! First-hand information, no need for guessing, interpretations or parallel evaluations. All we have to do is to let the Spirit help us. To do that we need to be followers of Jesus Christ and children of God by repenting of our transgressions and accept Jesus as our Lord and Saviour. The Father will then send the Holy Spirit to indwell within us and be our guide, councellor and magnify Scripture for us.

SEEKING PROTECTION FROM GOD ··············

As we study the Old Testament, it becomes very obvious that God occasionally gets angry and becomes very destructive. Remember the Flood, during which He wiped out all living beings except Noah, his family and one pair of each animal? He also blasted Sodom and Gomorrah off the map with fire and brimstone. After that, He caused plagues and the death of all Egyptian first-borns, to convince Pharaoh to release His people. Pharaoh let the Hebrews go, but then chased them with his army. So God eliminated his whole army in the Red Sea.

Consider Adam and Eve; they eat some fruit from a tree God said not to touch, and He kicked them out of Eden and made life difficult, accompanied by aging and death.

So continue many more stories of God's wrath upon those who do not do His will. After reading all this, who would not want to seek protection from God?

The New Testament is not quite as bad, but there was the time God eliminated 185,000 troops of the Assyrian army attacking Jerusalem. If God was on your side, you won; if not, you lost. No discussion, just action.

Then enters little baby Jesus with his mother Mary. They seem so innocent, harmless and loving. Who would be afraid of them? Even as Jesus grew up, he became a man of love, peace and joy. He would often say, "If you have seen me you have seen the Father" (John 14:7). But this is not really the image most people have of Big Daddy!

Scriptures also note that if one breaks any of God's commandments, they are condemned to eternal death. No wonder people are drawn to Mary the Mother of Jesus and to Jesus Himself. They are more like us and can understand our problems. We can talk to them. In some way or other, they can protect us from The Father, plead our case of for being human! We try hard but we slip up once and a while. All we need is a little forgiveness!

Continuing in the Scriptures, we come to the description about the End Times and the Great White Throne Judgment, where people are tormented for seven years and then a few are chosen to go to Heaven, while the rest of the world goes to Hell along with Satan and all his demons. This is serious stuff. Even the Bible states, *"... work out your salvation with fear and trembling"* (Philippians 2:12). The Book of Psalms says, *"The fear of the Lord is the beginning of wisdom"* (Psalm 111:10). Ok, we fear the Lord; now what do we do? Wouldn't the natural thing be to seek protection wherever we can?

Many different ways have been developed by various cultures to seek protection from God. Some make sacrifices to appease their gods. Others give money to the church hoping this will save them. Still others search out Mary, mother of Jesus, as their advocate. Some turn to Jesus, who was crucified for our sins so that we may be set free. Jesus is their protection from God's judgment. Others rely on the Holy Spirit as their guide and councellor. There are those who turn to Scripture and claim the promises given there. A few use their church sacraments as their assurance of protection. Many claim their good deeds in helping others, and their many works for society—they have been good, productive people. How could God the Father not accept all those who have honored Him in their own way?

There are numerous Scriptures that can be studied to try and understand God and our fear of God, each slightly different in content and implication. The one I relate to is Jesus' statement,

Not everyone who says to me, "Lord, Lord," will enter the kingdom of heaven, but only he who does the will of my Father who is in heaven. Many will say to me on that day, "Lord, Lord, did we not prophesy in your name, and in your name drive out demons and perform many miracles?" Then I will tell them plainly, "I never knew you. Away from me, you evildoers!" (Matthew 7:21–23).

Also read Matthew 25:34,41:

Then the King will say to those on his right, "Come, you who are blessed by my Father, take your inheritance, the kingdom prepared for you since the creation of the world…" Then he will say to those on his left, "Depart from me, you who are cursed, into the eternal fire prepared for the devil and his angels."

Also note,

Salvation is found in no one else [Jesus Christ], *for there is no other name under heaven given to men by which we must be saved* (Acts 4:12).

John wrote in his gospel,

But these are written that you may believe that Jesus is the Christ, the Son of God, and that by believing you may have life in his name (John 20:30–31).

These passages point to Jesus Christ as our way to Salvation and Eternal Life. Jesus does not protect us from God; rather, He cleanses us so we can be children of God, in order to receive His inheritance.

BIRTH AND DEATH ················

There are two aspects of our existence we have little control over, birth and death; yet they are the defining points on the timeline of our life. Most of our thought, effort and energy is spent living between these two points in time and space. There is not much time spent pondering what we were before our birth, nor what we will become after our death. For most, their total focus is on the here and now. Many consider birth a statistical, random event with little purpose other then the continuation of species, and death is not far from that. Thus, it is not unexpected that when the subject of our universe is discussed, the same general thoughts prevail on its birth and death. This puts the whole issue of creation and demise into a category of insignificance. Are we perhaps missing something, the whole meaning and significance of life and our existence?

I find it interesting that we put so much emphasis on life and so little on what was before and what continues after death. At birth, we have a celebration of the blessed event with all our family and friends involved at this joyous time. At death, we celebrate all the deceased has done in his or her lifetime, again involving our family and friends, this time mourning the passing. At birth, we look toward the future and all the possibilities. At death, we look back on all the accomplishments. Is this all there is to life? Like an actor coming on stage, performing lines, and then leaving with the curtains closing behind them—the show is over! If that is all there is to The Story of Life, then we are but sad players on this stage, for the end is known before we begin.

But wait! We are leaving out the Creator of all existence and life, the Ancient of Days who existed before there was a universe and who will continue after our physical world no longer exists. He has a lot to tell us about life before birth and after death and, as a matter of fact, about the life we are to live while on earth. Consider the following Scriptures, detailing first the time before birth, then after death:

Before I formed you in the womb I knew you, before you were born I set you apart; I appointed you as a prophet to the nations (Jeremiah 1:5).

When I was woven together in the depths of the earth, you eyes saw my unformed body. All the days ordained for me were written in your book before one of them came to be (Psalm 139:15–16).

For those God foreknew he also predestined to be conformed to the likeness of his Son, that he might be the first born among many brothers. And those he predestined, he also called; those he called, he also justified; those he justified, he also glorified (Romans 8:29–30).

For he chose us in him before the creation of the world to be holy and blameless in his sight. In love he predestined us to be adopted as his sons through Jesus Christ, in accordance with his pleasure and will—to the praise of his glorious grace, which he has freely given us in the One he loves… In him we were also chosen, having been predestined according to the plan of him who works out everything in conformity with the purpose of his will, in order that we, who were the first to hope in Christ, might be for the praise of his glory (Ephesians 1:4,5,11,12).

For we know in part and we prophesy in part, but when perfection comes, the imperfect disappears. Now we see but a poor reflection as in a mirror, then we shall see face to face. Now I know in part; then I shall know fully, even as I am fully known (1 Corinthians 13:9,10,12).

In my Father's house are many rooms; if it were not so, I would have told you. I am going there to prepare a place for you. And if I go and prepare a place for you, I will come back and take you to be with me that you also may be where I am (John 14:2,3).

I declare to you, brothers, that flesh and blood cannot inherit the kingdom of God, nor does the perishable inherit the imperishable. Listen, I tell you a mystery: We shall not all sleep, but we will all be changed—in a flash, in the twinkling of an eye, at the last trumpet. For the trumpet will sound, the dead will be raised imperishable, and we will be changed. For the perishable must clothe itself with the imperishable, and the mortal with immortality (1 Corinthians 15:50–53).

Before birth, we await our turn to come on the world's stage and play our part. During life on earth we learn what life is all about and who is the Creator of all life. It is a role of preparation for all that lies ahead in eternity. By our free will we choose to follow our Creator or to follow the Prince of this World, Satan. At death, our destiny is determined—either to be with God in Heaven for all eternity, praising Him for all He is and has done for us, or, to be cast apart from God into Hell, reserved for Satan and all who follow him. God has pre-ordained our timing and human potential, but we must work out our salvation with fear and trembling, for our future depends upon it.

RUNNING FROM GUILT ·············

When I think of guilt from a general perspective, I have no problems with it. After all, I am a reasonable person, trying to do good as best I can. When I can help someone, I enjoy doing it. When I have an accident, I always say, "I am sorry" to the person involved, and really mean it. Thus, in the day-to-day adventures in life, guilt is not a big deal for me. However, when I come to specific events where things went wrong, I still ponder if there was something I could have done, or should have done to prevent things from going awry. There is the haunting feeling that maybe, in some way, I was guilty of not doing more. Why didn't I have just the right answer or do the right thing? Is this the black cloud of guilt hanging in my subconscious? I had done the best I could do at the moment, but that was not good enough. The problems were not resolved and bad things happened. How do I get rid of these guilty feelings? Run away from them?

About a month or so ago a cousin, Steve, committed suicide; he shot himself in the head. He was about forty years old and had been at a number of our family get-togethers for Thanksgiving, Christmas, and Easter. At the time, I had not noticed anything unusual that would have caused a concern. From all logical perspectives, there is no way I could have known. Still, there is that concern that pops up, "Maybe I could have made a difference." I generally am so wrapped up in my projects that I do not pay much attention to other people and their problems.

As age slowly creeps up, my short-term memory is slipping. As a result, a number of things people expect do not get done. I just forget them. I really do not want to forget, but that part of the system is not working well. I am disappointed about not doing the things I said I would do and the people involved are disappointed about the whole thing. Therein lies another source of the guilt complex. Maybe I should write everything down? But when I do that, I forget where I put the note I wrote it on. Sometimes, my wife will get me started on a project, something will happen, and I will forget all about what I was doing and go off in another direction. Needless to say, she is disappointed. And, so am I. What to do with all these buckets of guilt?

I like the way Paul describes this situation in the Book of Romans, 7:21–25,

> *So I find this law at work; When I want to do good, evil is right there with me. For in my inner being I delight in God's law; but I see another law at work in the members of my body, waging war against the law of my mind and making me a prisoner of the law of sin at work within my members. What a wretched man I am! Who will rescue me from this body of death? Thanks be to God— through Jesus Christ our Lord.*

Jesus has said for us to come to Him with our burdens of sin, guilt and shame and He will set us free. We no longer need to run away from our guilt. Jesus has paid it all.

So, I have done that, I have gone to Jesus with these things. Why do they keep coming back? For a number of reasons; one is that we cannot erase our memories automatically. Thus, each time they come up, we must give them back to Christ again and again. A second reason is that Satan loves to torment us, and accuse us of being unworthy when things go wrong, all the while tempting us to think we are gods and can or should fix everything and make it right. A third reason is that we do genuinely love people and want the best for them, but we do not always *know* what is the best for them. It may not be what we think.

The last reason involves our self image—our pride, motivations, ambitions and reputations. These, too, can get in our way as leftovers from our Original Sin nature. They all cause us to run from guilt and turning everything over to Jesus Christ.

We cannot run and hide from our guilt. What a large burden we often carry about with us. Daily, if not more often, we must stop and turn this burden over to Jesus, who is eager to help us to get back on the path that leads to eternal life and being in Heaven with Him forever.

PRAYER IS THE LANGUAGE OF OUR DEPENDENCY ·················

Over time we develop many different languages. At work I used a scientific language with all the technical terms. Most people do not understand this language. This is typical for all the various professions, however; each develops its unique language. The sports world has their own language and so it goes in many specializations. Even my wife has her special language of feelings which is always a puzzle for me. I have difficulty with feelings, so it should be expected that I do not fully understand the language of feelings. In general we do not pay special attention to all these various languages, and they are not taught in our schools.

The arts possess another special set of languages. We are all familiar with the language of music and the many different dialects. Yet paintings and sculpture also have a special language each. I have often looked at a modernistic painting and wondered what the artist was trying to say. To me, the art does not make any sense; I do not understand that language.

Then there is the language of children—the young to the older. It begins with needs, then expression of feelings, on to wants and desires and finally to thoughts, observations, and opinions.

For language to exist, there must be a common understanding, some basis for expressing our consciousness. Consider the techniques of communications by special codes (languages). I've spent some time working with encryption systems and coding technology. Without having the Code Book, it was very difficult to "break" the code (or language), but it can be done. Even computers use special languages in binary code words; there are many of them. Our world is full of special languages.

Each family, tribe, culture, nationality and species has its peculiar language that has developed. These languages have changed down through the ages. It seems that each high school class has to develop its unique word meanings and language styles. There is something about our identity associated with the languages we use. The use of language is one way to show our unity and independence at the same time. We may look alike, but our languages are different.

In the physical domain we talk about the language of the heart, the language of love, the language of reason and logic, the language of observations, the language of emotion, the language of feelings, the language of imagination, the language of dreams, the language of the subconscious, the language of humor and so on.

In the spiritual domain we consider the language of worship, the language of prayer, the language of meditation, the language of God's Word, and the language God uses to communicate with us. These are different than the physical languages because they are living, eternal and powerful. The language of worship conveys wonder, majesty, honor, glory, love, and submission. The language of prayer is one of petition, need and thanksgiving—the recognition of our dependency upon God. The language of meditation is open, expectant and searching. The language of God's Word comes alive with meaning and impact to our lives far beyond just the physical words on the page; they become living words, and remind us of our needs and God's provisions. The common basis for these communications is the Holy Spirit that dwells within us. Without the Holy Spirit, we do not have a basis for understanding the spiritual languages. Also, the Holy Spirit speaks for us to God, expressing our most inner needs and feelings. For those who do not have the Holy Spirit, the spiritual language is meaningless, just empty words without power. They do not have the key to unlock the language.

In the physical world of languages, we express our independence, our uniqueness and our significance. In the spiritual world of languages, we express our dependencies, our commonness and our insignificance. We are totally dependent upon God for our creation, our maintenance, and our inspiration for life, which is reflected in our spiritual language, and most obvious in our prayers.

FAITH, THE PHYSICAL AND THE SPIRITUAL ⋯

I do not often bother to distinguish between my physical and spiritual faith. In the process I run into a lot of confusion and frustration. This confusion also applies to truth, belief, eternity, hope, love and other such words, where they can have both physical and spiritual meaning. For one thing, I do not have the same observations, understanding, and knowledge of the spiritual and physical. I am far more in the physical domain than in the spiritual domain. All my existence has been in the physical domain, with only occasional transitions into the spiritual, which were questionable, at best. Do we have any basis to say that there is a difference? Are both the same in any way?

Consider the Scriptural passage in which Jesus is talking to His disciples:

> *I tell you the truth, if you had the faith as small as a mustard seed, you can say to this mountain, "Move from here to there" and it will move. Nothing will be impossible for you* (Matthew 17:20–21).

I have read and studied that passage many times. The mustard seed was considered the smallest of seeds. How can it be that such an incredibly small amount can have such powerful results? Now, if we could generate spiritual faith like this on our own, we would not have need for knives, spears, bows and arrows, guns or atomic weapons. Also, I am sure that Jesus could move mountains. After all, what is that compared to the creation? During that process, massive galaxies were moved. God was very merciful in limiting our spiritual faith; it saves us from killing ourselves.

Read Ephesians,

For it is by grace you have been saved, through faith—and this not from yourselves, it is the gift of God—not by works, so that no one can boast (Ephesians 2:8–9).

It is through spiritual faith, this great power we do not understand, that salvation comes. It is not our own generated faith—we cannot generate any spiritual faith—it is a gift we receive from God. If we could generate our own spiritual faith, there would have been no reason for Jesus to come to earth and be sacrificed for our sins. We could have saved ourselves!

Also consider Matthew 9:21:

She said to herself, "If I only touch his cloak, I will be healed." Jesus turned and saw her. "Take heart, daughter," he said, "your faith has healed you" and the woman was healed from that moment.

God occasionally gives us faith of action; if we will do something, then what we may be desperately searching for will be given us. There is not a single formula. It is the initial spiritual faith that gets us to try again, to have confidence in success.

Consider also James 2:18, *"Show me your faith without deeds, and I will show you my faith by what I do."* If we have spiritual faith, there must be results. God does not give us faith to hang on the walls or store in the closet. We are given spiritual faith for specific tasks God wants us to accomplish. There is mountain-moving power in faith. There is salvational power in faith. There is healing power in faith. If spiritual faith were like ordinary physical faith, such as our faith that the sun will rise or a chair will hold us, there would be no supernatural power in it.

Now, for a few thoughts on the other words I mentioned at the beginning of this essay: truth, belief, eternity, absolute, hope and love. If it is physical truths we seek, we can generally find the answer to our confusion in the physical sciences. There is physical power in using these physical truths. However if these truths are spiritual, we have God's Word in the Bible and the indwelling of the Holy Spirit to guide us.

We have many beliefs, but specifically consider our belief in God. We can look at the physical universe around us and conclude that God must exist. However, if we have a spiritual belief, we have a relationship with God; we believe because we have met Him.

We have many physical hopes, but we have no assurance that they will ever be fulfilled. However, our spiritual hopes are based on Scriptures, and we are assured that they will certainly be fulfilled.

Physical love is very fickle and temporal. However, spiritual love gives us an energy that overflows, and we can do things we could never have done in our physical nature.

Next consider "absolute" and "eternity" from a physical basis. There may be very few things that are absolute (I include the laws of physics, but they are constantly being modified and improved), and the physical is not eternal. It is only in the spiritual domain we find the absolute and eternal, because that is the nature of the spiritual domain. Perhaps these differences defined will begin to help us understand the nature of the physical and spiritual worlds.

SUBJECTIVE TRUTH VERSUS OBJECTIVE TRUTH •••••••••••••

Truth is truth, so what difference does it make? My truth is different from another's truth because we all have different paths and perspectives as we go through life. I use my truth in my domain and others use their truth in their domain. As long as we each respect each other's domains, there is no conflict with our truths. The effectiveness of our truth is dependent upon the authority and persuasion each of us have. In this system it does not matter if our truth is objective or subjective for we are the ones enforcing or interpreting it.

Thus it would follow that those in greater authority have greater influence with their subjective truth; that is, we are subject to their truth. It does not matter what our subjective truth is; those in authority are dedicated to promoting their truth. In fact, many groups, companies and political parties spend significant money on trying to convince us that their subjective truth is really the objective truth. I wonder if they really know any objective truth, or could tell the difference between subjective and objective truth?

Objective truth is God's Word. It is not subject to any changes, revisions, updates, new insights, or higher authority. At God's Word, all of creation must obey, from the highest angels down to the lowest one-cell animal and even the smallest subatomic particle. Now that is objective truth! Any thing less is subjective truth. How can that be? For one consideration, it was by God's Word that everything was created. God spoke His Word and so it was done. Now, that is Truth with Power.

In addition, Jesus used God's Word when responding to Satan (Matthew 4:3–10). Each of Satan's challenges was stopped by Jesus responding with God's Word. Do we know how to use God's Word as our objective truth?

What could be more important then knowing God's Word when we are living in God's World? It is the authority and truth around which all creation revolves. Consider Jesus on the stormy sea with his disciples; one Word from Him and the wind and seas became still! (Matthew 8:23–26). Such is the power of God's objective truth in His Word.

Lest one get the false assumption that all we need to know are these "magic" words, and all this power is ours; consider the case of Simon the Sorcerer. He asked Peter to sell him the Spirit's power:

> *Peter responded, "May your money perish with you because you thought you could buy the gift of God with money!"* (Acts 8:20).

The second consideration is the objective truth in God's created universe. Our observations, experiments, measurements, and theories about the universe are but subjective truths. Note that we are continually changing our description and interpretations of these truths. It is also not unusual for people to disagree on the subjective truths of our universe, such as the purpose of life, what happens at physical death, how old the universe is, why things happen the way they do and what the end of the universe will be like. We have a limited source of God's objective truth on the universe. The Bible has little to say in scientific specifics, but does give general objective truths on the list above.

The third consideration of objective truth is the work of the Holy Spirit. This is probably more controversial than the first two areas, because our experience with the Holy Spirit is very subjective. Through the Holy Spirit—the third person of the Trinity of God—we subjectively experience objective truth. The Holy Spirit guides, counsels and interprets God's Word for our lives. The Spirit brings God's Word alive, active and powerful; there is an understanding that goes beyond the ordinary word, there is the power to change, there are directions for us to follow, and there are things for us to do. God's Word does not just sit on a page and look at us as we look at it; it is a living objective truth.

We have discussed the Trinity of Objective Truth; the Father originated the Word, the Son brought fulfillment of the Word, and the Spirit maintains the Word. May we let objective truth be our guide in this subjective world of ours.

THE INSEPARABLE BOUNDARIES ················

How often do we try to separate the inseparable? It may be as simple as salt in the sugar—just not worth the effort to separate them grain by grain—or as complex as separating the visible from the invisible, such as the visible electromagnetic light-waves from the radio or x-ray light-waves. There are ways we can do these things that may not be as trivial. There are additional areas where we cannot even imagine how to separate them. What are these inseparable boundaries that we must deal with from time to time? Let us consider a few metaphysical ones; physical and spiritual, mortal and immortal, and soul and spirit and God the Father, God the Son and God the Holy Spirit.

Some will take the simple position, "If I cannot see it, it does not exist!" This can be a very dangerous step as there are many things that are invisible that can kill us. Others may take the position of the majority of society, "The separation of Church and State is necessary!" or "Religion is a personal matter, keep it to yourself!" or "We do not want to see or hear anything that has to do with God!" The basic situation here is applying a linear reasoning to a nonlinear problem. The assumption is that these issues are readily separable, but they are not. So what do we do?

First, let us consider the inseparable boundaries between the physical and spiritual. We see the physical; we can measure it and weigh it and do something with it. Now, if the physical has a spiritual aspect, which many refuse to accept, there is very little we can do about that because we do not directly see any spiritual connection. There is no way to explain the existence of our universe as we cannot produce something from nothing; some entity other than a physical being has to be involved. We have chosen to call this Creator being, God. The fundamental connection to all matter comes from God. God is a Spirit living in the spiritual domain, thus everything has a spiritual connection—whatever that may mean. From our perspective, the physical and spiritual are inseparable. It is meaningless for us to try to separate them. But some will try.

Next, consider the separation between the mortal and immortal. There are two definitions, one physical and one spiritual (there we are again). After they are dead, we speak of famous people's works as their immortal works, but that is only in a physical sense. The Bible states that each person has an immortal soul, it does not die when we die physically. That is, we continue to exist as a spiritual being, unique and identifiable as ourselves with all our memories after death, and reside in the spiritual domain. Thus we are both mortal and immortal.

However, not everything has an immortal existence. Can we separate that which does and that which does not? Or which souls are bound for Heaven and which are off to Hell? These things are inseparable.

Further consider soul and spirit. Who is able to separate soul from spirit? The best we might do is identify our soul as our eternal essence, personality and memories—our non-physical parts—and our spirit part as our connection and communications with God—the indwelling of the Holy Spirit. Scriptures note,

> For the word of God is living and active. Sharper than any double-edge sword, it penetrates even to dividing soul and spirit... (Hebrews 4:12).

Lastly, we come to the Trinity; Father, Son and Spirit. What a stumbling block for all those who have made the valiant attempt to separate the inseparable, not to mention those who have tried to understand what the first group has said or written. What is it about ourselves that we must divide and conquer? Yes, without separation, we cannot define what an object is, in order to give it a unique description and identity (and try to control it). Yet what if there are elements not definable in physical terms? Things that are invisible, eternal or spiritual cannot be described with physical words or expressions. Nevertheless, we continue trying to define them.

Many would consider love as inseparable boundary, at least that is the promise of wedding vows, but the statistics are not good. Human love can be very fickle. The love of God is a different matter altogether; Paul wrote,

> *For I am convinced that neither death nor life, neither angels nor demons, neither the present nor the future, nor any powers, neither height nor depth, nor anything else in all creation, will be able to separate us from the love of God that is in Christ Jesus our Lord* (Romans 8:38,39).

Now, the love of God we can count on, and is an inseparable boundary for those who love Him.

THE SPIRITUAL ECOSYSTEM ···············

We have all heard about the physical ecosystem, but what about a spiritual ecosystem? What can that be? Let us first consider the physical ecosystem, and then look for a parallel in the spiritual domain.

What is an ecosystem? Webster's Dictionary states that the word "eco" or "ec" is from the Greek "oik" meaning house or household; presently used as habitat or environment. Thus we think of an ecosystem as the ordered procedures and processes in our habitat or environment. These are things we experience daily and we have developed an understanding of their operations and requirements.

The purpose of the distinction between the physical and spiritual ecosystem is to gain insight into the contributions of and interrelationships between these two ways of analysis.

Now, the physical ecosystem is concerned with rules, roles and rituals based on maintaining a stable system. The spiritual ecosystem focuses on relationships, resources and revelations with concerns for growth and adaptation to changes. Another way of looking at this is that the physical ecosystem relates to how it works whereas the spiritual ecosystem looks to why it works. For example, an examination and evaluation of a physical ecosystem may reveal that the system is surviving, shrinking or spreading. This is all valuable information for projecting performance, but it provides little in terms of what is causing these results. On the other hand, the spiritual ecosystem tries to understand the basis for existence, energy and endurance. The evaluations are: is it essential, is it effective and is it efficient? It is more a dynamic living system than a static, mechanical system.

The sciences are well-suited to examining, evaluating and expressing the physical aspects of any ecosystem. The tools and techniques are well-developed, and even further specialized into many different departments of sciences with incredible depth of understanding. However, when we come to the spiritual domain, we find a much different condition. Very little is known or understood, and there is rarely agreement on the views of different groups regarding the elements studied. For the purpose of this discussion, we shall be using the Christian perspective.

In a fundamental way, the physical ecosystems represent the world the way it is now—a system generally described as a random in evolution, statistical in nature and lacking in meaning; that is, a system without purpose, direction or cause. This is a condition the Scriptures describe as a Fallen World and under the domination of Satan and his demonic followers. As such, we have a very confused, complex and contradicting ecosystem, originally created by God, but fallen into chaos and condemnation because of rebellion against its Creator. The model of such an ecosystem is aptly described by the Second Law of Thermodynamics as a system in decay and death. Such a system is basically unstable and constantly accelerating to higher levels of confusion and disorder.

As a counter-system, the spiritual ecosystem represents the world as it should be, with God in full control—a system with a single purpose and direction, stable and eternal. It is the achievement of "Heaven on Earth," which is prophesied for the future when Jesus Christ returns to earth. The basic challenge for us who live in this present world is to understand God's purpose and direction, for this produces a spiritual ecosystem that will really work, since it will have the direction, control and power of the Holy Spirit behind it. There is no greater source than God, the Father, the Son and the Holy Spirit. God created the universe to glorify Himself, not to glorify us. For what glory is in us, as all we are and have has been given to us by our Father in Heaven?

So what do we do with these two perspectives? The process is to synthesize an approach that utilizes the temporal and imperfect to implement the perfect purposes and goals of our Father. We need a synergetic combination of the physical with the spiritual, whereby the spiritual is always in control and not the other way around. We need to accomplish this synthesization to the best of our ability, as we rely on Scripture, prayer, meditation and the Holy Spirit for guidance, wisdom and power. What other way is there that leads to life as God intends? Who could imagine building a perfect kingdom out of imperfect materials?

There is yet hope; the "magic" transformation completed at physical death, where the mortal takes on immortality—the restoration of The Fall.

HOW TO COMMIT SUICIDE ···············

It seems that everyone these days wants the right to end their life; not that they are planning on doing it right away. If things get tough, they want a way out. Dr. Kavorkian was very popular with his program to help those die who had lost all hope of recovering their health. The Netherlands has been very progressive in approving euthanasia for its population. It is well-known that many elderly people stop eating and even drinking water, which rapidly accelerates death; this is most often associated with terminal stages of illness; the desire for food and water is lost. We might call this a natural approach to committing suicide. There are many ways to accelerate one's death, accidentally, naturally or intentionally. Yet there is another way to look at this basic problem.

Remember that Adam and Eve were the first ones to commit suicide. We did not originate the idea. God told them,

You are free to eat from any tree in the garden; but you must not eat from the tree of the knowledge of good and evil, for when you eat of it you will surely die (Genesis 2:16–17).

So what did they do? They went out and ate the fruit of this tree. That is like someone saying to us, "if you eat this arsenic pill you will die"; then another tries to convince us we won't die, so we go and eat the arsenic pill. Guess what? We die! Does it really make a difference that someone tried to convince us we really would not die? It seems to me we've been through that with cigarette smoking, when the Surgeon General said smoking was hazardous to health and could cause death. The cigarette industry said, Don't believe that, it has not been proven. So many kept on smoking and dying. What is it with people? Are we born with a death wish? It gets worse when we think of all the wars, terrorists acts and violent criminals there have been, still are and will be.

It is true that we all are going to die. Just being alive is an indication that we are in the process of committing suicide. It is just a matter of how long it is going to take and how it is going to happen. Some people commit suicide by working hard; they forget there are limitations and maintenance requirements for the human body. Others like to defy the laws of statistics, or the laws of nature such as gravity, or of civilization, which bring on the death penalty. Just different ways of committing suicide? What about driving our car or taking a trip on an airplane? Each of these and many more things we do each day are potential ways of committing suicide, because we make the choice to do them. To live is to risk dying; suicide is just a matter of definition. We may classify something as suicide, but those doing it just consider it having fun, excitement, adventure, duty or harmless activity.

Let us consider further the Word of God. If we break His commandments, the penalty is spiritual death; we can consider this spiritual suicide. Most people pay no or very little attention to God's commandments, and in that way commit spiritual suicide every day. Jesus Christ, God's Son, came on a suicide mission to earth, to sacrifice His life as a ransom to pay our sin debt of death to God the Father.

Jesus said to her [Martha], *"I am the resurrection and the life. He who believes in me will live, even through he dies; and whoever lives and believes in me will never die.*

Do you believe this?" (John 11:25–26).

Consider also what Jesus said,

"Enter through the narrow gate. For wide is the gate and broad is the road that leads to destruction, and many enter through it. But small is the gate and narrow the road that leads to life, and only a few find it." (Matthew 7:14).

Sounds to me like the wide gate and broad path are suicide. Life in Jesus Christ is the small gate and narrow road to spiritual life and eternity.

Perhaps, if we looked at life, both the physical and spiritual, from a perspective of committing suicide, we may choose a different direction for the life God has given us.

Then Jesus said to his disciples, "If anyone would come after me, he must deny himself and take up his cross and follow me. For whoever wants to save his life will lose it, but whoever loses his live for me will find it. What good will it be for a man if he gains the whole world, yet forfeits his soul?" (Matthew 16:24–26).

Jesus is saying we must commit a suicide of self to be able to receive the Holy Spirit to dwell within us, and to gain eternal life.

THE FORGOTTEN PERSPECTIVE ⋯⋯⋯⋯⋯⋯

Our churches emphasize the Bible as the main source of knowledge about God. Now this is very good, but then we can only study what God as done from creation up to about 100 A.D. Even this is very limited to following the genetic line from Adam and Eve up to Jesus Christ; primarily the early history of the Jews. Can we really assume that the Bible is the only source we need? For the other developments in the world during this time period, we must rely on the various sciences trying to put the pieces together, and on a very few historians.

The period from 100 A.D. to the present 2001 A.D. is primarily left for the secular historians to analyze and record the major events, and for the scientists to discover the laws of our universe. The problem I see is that all spiritual aspects, the interactions of God, and God as Creator, are left out. Now there are church historians who primarily focus on the church and its development, but their studies are generally related to a specific denomination. Thus, when we try to understand who we are, where we have been, and where we are going, we are largely dependent upon secular interpretations and viewpoints. I recall taking a required, very rigorous year-long class in college on Western Civilization. Very little time was spent on the role of churches and religions, and I do not recall any discussion of God.

Being able to know and understand history is very important. Consider the many wars that have occurred, the reasons for them, the impact on countries involved, and the long-term results.

Financially, there have been major swings from boom to bust. There are many things that effect the financial market; it is important to know the "signs of the time."

Weather-wise, we have gone from major cold spells to significant warming trends. Such changes as El Niño (the warming trend in the ocean currents), the sun spot eleven year cycles (did we realize that there was a seventy-year period when there were no sun spot cycles? Those were very cold years), and major changes in the rain cycles from dry to wet years.

We have tried many times to end all wars through organizations like The League of Nations and United Nations, but they have failed. Many have tried to predict the financial markets, and they too have failed. We are not yet to the point of being able to accurately predict the weather, or even understand all the elements and factors that effect the weather. Where we cannot predict the future accurately, we then need to rely on history to understand the trends and cycles of the world around us so we may be prepared. Essentially, all of these historic data have been subject to secular analysis and evaluation. The possibility of God being involved in the care and maintenance of His creation has not been considered in the process. The Scriptures note that all things are under God's control; nothing happens without God allowing it to happen. Therefore all that we call history was under God's control and followed His plan.

As we listen to the" news," enjoy our material accumulations and marvel at the technology breakthroughs, we can easily forget and miss all that God is doing. How can we thank God and give Him the honor and glory He deserves if we only look at history through secular perspectives? We may complain about the present interpretations and implementations of the separation of Church and State, but what about the separation of God and history? If we believe the modern teachings, God is not involved in our current world. He was only active for the Jews, and even that was way back before 100 A.D..

Now we come to a serious problem. Many have turned to God in prayer and asked for His blessings to get us through the impact and destruction of the terrorist attacks of September 11, 2001. Yet can we also accept that God allowed this to happen? Will we be able to see that God will take this great, evil event and turned it into something wonderfully good? How big is our vision of God? Can we give Him the glory, honor and praise for being our God during these difficult times, as well as during the easy times? I do not know how God is going to transform the events of September 11, but I am sure He will. It will be a God-sized transformation. Praise our Lord in all circumstances!

....

CHAPTER 4

Applications of Science to Our Nonphysical World

M y basic love is science, the eternal search for the answers to "Why?" This started when I was very young and is still a strong drive in my life today. The specific focus has changed with time, but an education in the sciences and a background of over thirty-five years in research and development has laid a good foundation for the continued search to answer the question, "Why?"

> Jesus Christ is end of all, and the center to which all tends.
> Whoever knows Him knows the reason of everything.
>
> Blaise Pascal (1623–1662)

> God does not play dice with the universe.
>
> Albert Einstein

God could have made the universe in a different way. That is, whether the necessity of logical simplicity leaves any freedom at all.

John P. Barrow, *Theory of Everything*

THE BURDEN OF OUR FALLEN WORLD ··········

Can we possibly imagine the burden our fallen world must endure? Probably not. What could we use as our reference point? For those who carefully read the Bible, there are a few passages that give some hints as to what this may all be about. Let us consider the following:

> *To Adam he said, "Because you listened to your wife and ate from the tree about which I commanded you, 'you must not eat of it,' Cursed is the ground because of you; though painful toil you will eat of it all the days of your life. It will produce thorns and thistles for you, and you will eat the plants of the field. By the sweat of your brow you will eat your food until you return to the ground, since from it you were taken; for dust you are and to dust you will return"* (Genesis 3:17–19).

In our garden I find not only "thorns and thistles," but gophers, moles, ants, aphids, spiders, moths, along with many, many weeds. The plants and trees we do want grow out of control and need continual trimming. Some plants in our garden are good for just one season and then must be replanted in the spring. The grass grows and needs frequent mowing and occasional fertilizer. In the fall, the trees drop their leaves (or pine needles) and that is a big clean-up operation. During a big storm once, we had a pine tree and part of our fence blow over. All in all, our garden is a lot of work to keep it in shape. I believe these are all aspects of the Fall. But what about the physical cause?

We can all agree that the perfect garden should not have these problems; perhaps it is a case of things gone out of balance? The CO_2 level in the atmosphere has a lot to do with plant growth, as photosynthesis changes CO_2 and water into O_2 and plant sugars. The more CO_2, the more growth—both the rate and type of growth. Thus, the basic nature of plants could change with differences in carbon dioxide levels.

There is evidence that the earth has changed its rotational axis, revealed, over past times, in the magnetic polarization of lava flows. Thus, we may now have very different seasonal weather conditions than first existed. A more even temperature and, perhaps, constant sun illumination may have existed. Consider, *"The Lord God made garments of skins for Adam and his wife and clothed them"* (Genesis 3:21). Why exactly did they need clothes after the Fall, when they did not need them before? The general interpretation is that it was to cover their nudity, in place of their fig leaves. However, another possibility could be that there was going to be a significant change in the weather!

The background cosmic and x-ray radiation from space can cause mutations in our chromosomes and other body cells; on the average each of us has about 100 chromosomes that have been damaged. We now have concerns about the ozone depletion over the Poles. Before the Flood, there was a canopy of "water" or clouds, which provided shielding.

> *In the six hundredth year of Noah's life, on the seventeenth day of the second month—on that day all the springs of the great deep burst forth, and the flood-gates of the heavens were opened. And the rain fell on the earth forty days and forty nights* (Genesis 7:11–12).

Now forty days of heavy rain takes many large clouds. It was also after this time that people's lives became shorter. But this was all after the Fall; it was another judgment on top of the first.

Earth models show all land was joined as a single unit in the beginning. Then, as the tectonic plates moved, the land was separated into different islands and regions. One might speculate that in the judgment of the Tower of Babel (Genesis 11), more than the separate languages were given to various people. Perhaps this was also the beginning of separate land masses. The development of species in these isolated regions became very specialized and different from each other. We have significantly altered these specializations by our rapid transportation and deportment of plants, animals and other life forms around the globe. Life would have been simpler before all these adaptations and intermixing took place.

The list continues with huge volcanic eruptions, great meteor impacts, massive glacier growth, a 300 (or more) foot drop in oceans, wide-spread forest fires, plagues and illnesses of all kinds, great destructive earthquakes, droughts and floods in various areas, and wild storms of wind and rain. Many of these are driven by forces within the earth, and off the earth—those exerted by the moon and the sun through gravity and the direct changes in the sun's radiated energy.

We must not neglect the psychological and other changes in Adam and Eve when God separated them from Himself. They no longer had direct spiritual access to God and His knowledge and wisdom. They now had to rely on their physical senses, knowledge and wisdom a lot more. This is often referred to as a spiritual death; God is a spirit and we can only communicate with Him in spirit. Thus our focus became more worldly directed.

One popular explanation of the Fall is the the Second Law of Thermodynamics; all processes in nature have losses—there are energy losses with each and every interaction. There are many mechanisms such as friction, radiation, conduction, noise and thermal effects, which eliminate the possibility of perpetual motion or a system lasting forever; everything is in a state of decay. A system goes from a higher order to a lower order and, eventually, there is no difference in temperature or energy level—a state of thermal death. In a world without losses, a ball would continue to bounce forever, a boat once pushed off from shore would continue to the other side without slowing down, and once the air started moving, it would not stop—it would be a strange world. It is not immediately obvious that the Second Law of Thermodynamics is God's curse, and responsible for all the above changes.

After all this discussion, what can we conclude? First, we can observe that there has been a sequence of judgments from God: first the Fall, then the Flood, followed by the Tower of Babel and, I would include, the events of Exodus, the Exile to Babylon and the Crucifixion and Resurrection of Jesus Christ. I would expect there have been more, as we look back to the Dark Ages, The Plague, W.W. I and II, and even the Cold War. One might even conclude today that we have the judgment of pollution as a major curse on our environment. The general assumption is that we have brought these judgments on ourselves. In place of prophets bringing us God's Word and Truth, we have politicians bringing us stories and half-truths.

With this perspective our fallen world becomes more burdensome each day. We continually add to the problem and, most often, do not realize we are doing it; it is all part of our fallen nature. God does not have to step in with major pronouncements of judgment, we do it to ourselves. We have reached the size and capacity that we can produce major crisis on the environment worldwide. What we need is God's help to get back to being good managers of His world.

The Scriptures describe the period of the Millennium as the time of Jesus Christ's Second Coming. He will rule on earth with an iron rod and all knees shall bow and all tongues confess that He is Lord of lords and King of kings. All things will be made right again, including our environment, and peace will prevail.

Yet there is the final judgment left to come, The Great Tribulation prophesied in Revelation; a most devastating and dreadful time to be alive. Many hold to the Rapture occurring before the Great Tribulation crescendo, the event when Jesus Christ comes in the air and removes His followers, The Church, from earth so they will not have to endure these terrible times.

There is not agreement on the exact order and timing of the Rapture, Tribulation, Millennium and the great war of Armageddon, but all these must come before we get to the final Great White Throne Judgment and the separation of sheep and goats, and then the coming of the New Heavens and New Earth and the New Jerusalem, which will exist into eternity. It will be a time when the mortal and temporal are transformed into the immortal and eternal by the resurrection power of God our Father. All will be new. There will be no more pain, suffering and death for that has passed away. The burden of our world will be lifted and the unbelievers sent to Hell.

Are the exact details and timing of these events important to our understanding of God and our having faith in Him? The basic message is that we are clueless, hopeless and powerless to dig ourselves out of the mess we have made of our world, without God coming to our rescue. For Him to come to us requires us to renounce our own wills and put all our hope, faith and love in God's Son, Jesus Christ, for that is the only way to our Salvation.

THE REAL AND THE IMAGINARY ··············

When I was in high school, our math teacher introduced us to the world of real and imaginary numbers. The imaginary numbers all had a "j" in front of them and we would write, "4 + j7," representing a real and imaginary part of the mathematical quantity. If a person multiplied two imaginary numbers together, the result was a negative real number; j7 x j5 = - 35. That was cool. Then, we would plot real and imaginary numbers on two dimensional graphs with the real number along the X axis and the imaginary along the Y axis; the two orthogonal directions on the paper. I had a ball playing with these real and imaginary numbers. We could then calculate the angle represented by these real and imaginary numbers using trigonometry. My mind went wild with all these new concepts, ideas and possibilities. Our world was really real and imaginary all at once!

The next few summers of college I worked for the San Diego Gas and Electric Company as a junior engineer. Guess what? I used real and imaginary numbers to calculate many different factors in analyzing electrical power transmission. We used power load factors which were real and imaginary numbers. These load factors represented the phase differences between voltage and current caused by inductive and capacitive loads. Since motors always had a large inductive load factor, we would put capacitors on the power lines to equalize the load factor. A large imaginary load factor would cause significant problems and produced ground currents in our standard three-phase power transmission lines. Yes, even the three-phase power lines were represented by real and imaginary numbers. I would go out in the field to observe powerline structures and, with the master grid charts, I would calculate the line-to-line and line-to-ground fault currents. I had more fun than one can imagine. Real and imaginary numbers were very important and useful. And I was paid for doing it all. The world could be represented by real and imaginary numbers!

Our minds are very creative and can produce many things. However, they are all imaginary. They are not real. To produce something new, we must combine the imaginary with real physical elements. We could describe everything as combinations of the real things, the atoms and sub-atomic particles, with everything being made from them as the imaginary component assemblies. These imaginary assemblies require intelligence. They show a pattern, a plan and a purpose which represents the intelligence. As intelligence is not physical and real, it must be imaginary: that which is orthogonal to the real. Now, that is a bit shocking as we are so accustomed to calling these things and beings made from atoms and sub-atomic particles real, physical entities. We do not directly see the atoms and sub-atomic particles since they are much too small. If we follow this logic, then everything we see is imaginary, the product of the intelligence assembling building blocks. The only thing real is the atomic and sub-atomic particles. (Sometimes I wonder about these as quantum mechanics describes these atomic, sub-atomic, nuclear and sub-nuclear particles as just wave functions with probability densities). However, there is another step in this process!

Scripture states that God is a spirit. Now, if anything is imaginary in our world, the spirit would certainly be at the top of the list. If God is a spirit, what is the mind of God? The imaginary part of the spirit? We have definite problems with an anthropomorphic representation of God. Perhaps this is why we struggle so, trying to understand the Bible.

The fact is, we really do not understand our own world or ourselves. Probably, if we really understood ourselves, we would have a better chance of understanding God. The Scriptures describe us as "we see but a poor reflection as in a mirror" (1 Corinthians 13:12). I think this is a great understatement. There is a very good chance that we have everything backwards. What we call "real" is really imaginary and what we call "imaginary" is really real. The Bible notes that we have a history of rebelling against God; what we call good is really evil and what we call evil is really good.

What are we to do? Scripture says that we are not to depend upon our own understanding—I think that is quite obvious. To depend upon every word of God as true and absolute is very hard to do. If it were not for the indwelling of the Holy Spirit, it would be an impossible task to understand the Word of God. I believe the above discussion proves this—QED (*quod erat demonstrandum,* which was to be demonstrated).

THE MIRRORS OF OUR MIND ....

Some consider our mind to have windows through which we view ourselves and the world we live in. To me, the views are more like reflections in mirrors, each having some degree of distortion which is not immediately recognized. Mirrors reflect images; we do not see things directly. The images in our mind bounce around from one mirror to another. Each mirror slightly changes the original image. Thus, as time progresses, the images slowly change. Some elements are magnified, some are reduced or even disappear from the scene. Are these effects real? Do we really not not "see" the full world around us?

Our eyes are sensitive to a very limited spectrum of light energy, specifically 3,800 to 7,600 Angstroms. Fortunately these wavelengths correspond to the peak light spectrum from the sun, and the low absorption region of our atmosphere. This spectrum covers about one billionth of the total spectrum of light; we call this "seeing." If a person sees but ten percent of what others see, we call them functionally blind! It turns out that our sight is more complicated than even this. The image the eye sensors receive is upside down and backwards, caused by the lens in our eye. No problem, however; one of the processes of the brain is to reverse this transformation. The brain does many other processing functions on the visual information. Our fastest response is motion detection—part of the fight or flight survival system. This loop bypasses all other sight processing. There is a series of steps in seeing: recognizing light levels, sectioning image, determination of textures and colors, edge enhancements, delineating shapes and recognizing patterns. For some reason, our vision is far more sensitive to straight lines than random shapes by a factor of about 200 times. Thus it can be concluded that what we "see" has undergone many transformations and is highly dependent upon our stored recognition patterns. This implies that everyone's "seeing" is different. Thus my rationale for the mirrors of our mind. But does this have any real or practical significance?

What is life? In part it is just a collection of our stored images. The one advantage of paintings, photographs and movies is that the images experience very little change over time. Thus, by looking at our collection, we can "refresh" the images bouncing around in our hall of mirrors.

There is another aspect to our mirrors; we can create our own images. We have a sense of what things should look like and create them. For example, many of the modern paintings do not reflect the real world. In the field of computer graphics and animation we can create moving images that could never exist in the real world, but they look real! We are continually being challenged to distinguish between the real and the imaginary. Going even further, there is the wide open field of visual illusions. One example is the magic tricks of the prestidigitators. Other examples relate to the processing characteristics of our eyes, such as seeing the complimentary colors of objects, the disappearance of an object at our blind spot, three-color partitioning and eye fatigue.

There is another mirror our mind can look at; it is our spiritual mirror. This mirror is sometimes bright and clear, but most of the time very opaque and dark. The spiritual world is a mystery because we do not "see" what is happening. It is easy to ignore these mirrors altogether. When we do study them, they give us insight to the meaning of all our other mirrors. Our spiritual mirrors are not limited to the physical space and time to which we are bound.

The Scriptures have several references to mirrors and reflections. Jesus said, *"Anyone who has seen me has seen the Father"* (John 14:9). Jesus totally reflected his Father just as one would see in a mirror; not physical, but in character and action. The objective of God is to have us become the likeness of His Son, Jesus. We are to reflect the image of Jesus who is reflecting the image of his Father. Paul discusses our seeing in 1 Corinthians 13:12,

> *Now we see but a poor reflection as in a mirror; then* [in heaven] *we shall see face to face. Now I know in part; then I shall know fully, even as I am fully known.*

Our spiritual mirrors do not reflect well here on earth.

Now, there are a lot of things that degrade mirrors; they need frequent maintenance. If not, distortions, blurry spots, absorbing dust films, and the discoloration of reflective surface can occur. We carefully clean the mirrors in our home at least once a week, sometimes more often when fingerprints and splash marks appear. The same thing can happen with our spiritual mirrors with worldly distractions, pride, and other sins. We need prayer, repentance, meditation and to study God's Word to keep them clean.

THE SPIRIT GENE SEARCH ················

Could the secret of our lives all be in our genes? If we know a person's genetic make-up, is, then, the person's nature predetermined? Just think, we could find the Islam gene, the Hindu gene, the Buddhist gene, the Jewish gene and the Protestant genes with all its variations. Perhaps we could even discover the cultist genes. Oh what progress we could make in evangelism; it would all be predetermined in the spirit genes! Is this really so far from reality? What do the Scriptures say about this?

> *Then God said, "Let us make man in our image, in our likeness, and let them rule over the fish of the sea and the birds of the air, over the livestock, over all the earth, and over all the creatures that move along the ground." So God created man in his own image, in the image of God he created him; male and female he created them* (Genesis 1:26).

Since God is a spirit, we might expect that, along with our physical genes, we may also have spiritual genes. Is there more? Then we have Adam and Eve's Fall:

> *And the Lord God commanded the man, "You are free to eat from any tree in the garden; but you must not eat from the tree of the knowledge of good and evil, for when you eat of it you will surely die"* (Genesis 2:17).

Satan deceived Eve and convinced her to eat the forbidden fruit. Adam and Eve did not physically die, so it must have been spiritually. They did receive the sinful nature genes. This is also supported by,

...Jesus declared, "I tell you the truth, no one can see the kingdom of God unless he is born again." "How can a man be born when he is old?" Nicodemus asked... Jesus answered, "I tell you the truth, no one can enter the kingdom of God unless he is born of water and the Spirit" (John 3:3–5).

Here we find the "death" of our spiritual nature or genes; then through Jesus Christ paying our sin debt, we can be reborn in our spiritual nature; our spiritual genes will be revived. Perhaps the use of "born again" is more applicable to our spiritual genes then to our physical body, as spirits do not have bodies. Obviously something must be the basis of the spiritual nature, so why not genes?

Next we have:

For if you live according to the sinful nature [genes], *you will die; but if by the Spirit you put to death the misdeeds of the body, you will live, because those who are lead by the Spirit of God are sons of God. For you did not receive a spirit that makes you a slave again to fear, but you received the Spirit of sonship* [spiritual genes]. *And by him we cry, "Abba, Father," The Spirit himself testifies with our spirit that we are God's children. Now if we are children, then we are heirs—heirs of God and co-heirs with Christ, if indeed we share in his suffering in order that we may also share in his glory* (Romans 8:13–17).

Being children of God would indicate that we have the spiritual genes of God's family. In place of a "blood" line, we have the "spirit" line of genes to be identified with God's family.

Now consider:

For those God foreknew he also predestined to be con-
formed to the likeness of his Son, that he might be the
firstborn among many brothers. And those he predes-
tined, he also called; those he called, he also justified;
those he justified, he also glorified (Romans 8:29–30).

Knowing our full gene composition would allow prediction of our future development, strengths, weaknesses,
and characteristics. The process of justification, sanctification and glorification can represent the development of our
spiritual genes.

Also we have:

So will it be with the resurrection of the dead. The body
that is sown is perishable, it is raised imperishable; it is
sown in dishonor, it is raised in glory; it is sown in weak-
ness, it is raised in power; it is sown a natural body, it is
raised a spiritual body (1 Corinthians 15:42–44).

Thus, if the natural body has a structure based on physical genes, then we may expect a parallel that our spiritual
body will have spiritual genes.

There should be a residual spiritual gene in our mortal
body that allows us to respond to the call of the Holy Spirit.
If we repent of our sins and follow Jesus as our Lord and
Saviour, we receive the Holy Spirit, regeneration of our spiritual gene, and thus become children of God. Those who
choose not to be born again in their spirit will die in their sin.
They are children of Satan and have his spiritual nature with
its fallen spiritual gene set.

THE SPIRITUAL GENE POOL MANAGEMENT ····

There is much evidence for connecting personalities, characteristics and disposition to specific genes. There is certainly physical resemblance in the family members. In addition, research has shown that infants respond much better to related family members than to random baby sitters. Throughout history families, tribes, groups, and nationalities have formed common bonds generally along related gene bases. There is a special research effort in Iceland as almost all the people there have very similar genes forming a common pool. Genetics research has produced major breakthrough in tracing the movement of peoples and establishing points of origin. Even more applications of gene research are expected. The science of cloning has been demonstrated and gene modification medicines for correcting bad genes is next. Where will it end?

If we know a person's genetic make-up, is their nature predetermined? There does seem to be reasonable evidence that family characteristics continue in future generations. Doctors are most concerned about the medical history of other family members. There are concerns that personal gene information may be used by companies in hiring, and by insurance companies in setting their rates. I have not heard about it, but one might expect a gene analysis required for schools or colleges as they now use IQ and aptitude tests. The police are finding gene information often more useful than fingerprints. There are many gene pool management options for people, companies and governments.

Consider God's management of the human gene pool on earth. If it got contaminated, He created a disaster that wiped out the bad genes. Then consider the path from Adam and Eve up to the birth of Jesus. The Bible traces this very carefully and details the records of the Jews; in fact, they were called "The Chosen People." Basically, God chose a gene pool for His people. Scriptures note they were not to marry outside their gene pool. There were serious charges brought against those who "went after foreign wives." It would seem that even Satan got into the temptations of corrupting the gene pool by enticing other nations to send their young women over to the Hebrew men. Also, the Levites were chosen to be priests, again a form of gene pool control and specialization. In another area, Scripture notes,

> *You shall not make for yourself an idol in the form of anything in heaven above or on the earth beneath or in the waters below. You shall not bow down to them or worship them; for I, the Lord your God, am a jealous God, punishing the children for the sin of the fathers to the third and fourth generations of those who hate me, but showing love to a thousand generations of those who love me and keep my commandments* (Exodus 20:4–6).

This sounds like gene pool management to me.

What do the Scriptures say about our management of the spiritual gene pool?

> *Anyone who strikes a man and kills him shall surely be put to death. Anyone who attacks his father or his mother must be put to death. Anyone who kidnaps another and either sells him or still has him when he is caught must be put to death. Anyone who curses his father or mother must be put to death. If however, the bull has had the habit of goring and the owner has been warned but has*

*not kept it penned up and it kills a man or woman, the
bull must be stoned and the owner also must be put to
death. Anyone who has sexual relations with an animal
must be put to death. Observe the Sabbath, because it is
holy to you. Anyone who desecrates it must be put to
death...* (Exodus 21:12,15,16,17,21; 22:19; 31:14).

In the promised land, the Jews were to kill all the inhabitants and possess the land flowing with milk and honey—the
elimination of many gene pools. There are other passages
where gene pools have been removed by direction of God to
His people:

*"They may marry anyone they please as long as they
marry within the tribal clan of their father. No inheritance in Israel is to pass from tribe to tribe"* (Numbers
36:6–7).

*"A man is not to marry his father's wife; he must not dis-
honor his father's bed"* (Deuteronomy 22:30).

*"They must not marry widows or divorced women; they
may marry only virgins of Israelite descent or widows of
priests"* (Ezekiel 44:22).

*"Do not be yoked together with unbelievers. For what do
righteousness and wickedness have in common? Or what
fellowship can light have with darkness?"* (2
Corinthians 6:14).

God has also giving many instructions about gene pool
management.

THE SPIRITUAL GENE CLONING ···············

Now just think, what if we could find a scrap of Jesus' genes? From the Shroud of Sharon, perhaps, or some other source. We could clone Jesus! Oh, what history this would be! We could make our own second coming of Jesus Christ through cloning! Or, how many Jesus' would we like? What a breakthrough for religious science. We can be our own salvation! However, as we read Scripture, this is not how it is to happen. Yet, it could make a great novel and even movie for all those who like to capitalize on religion and spiritual things. Or, how much would people pay to have their very own Jesus child to raise and train as they would like? The mind can go wild with possibilities and adventures. If they could clone Jesus, they could also go back and do many of the other religious and world leaders. Oh, what a mess we could get ourselves into. Not to mention Satan having a second shot at tempting Jesus—we could end up with the Anti-Christ in place of Christ!

Imagine further; Jesus had a sinless nature, therefore not fallen as were Adam and Eve and we are! This could give the whole new possibility of a perfect race. We could do what Hitler could not do with the "superior" Aryan race. A slight problem in coming up with the perfect woman however; but that should be a minor hurdle for today's genetic sciences. The possibilities seem unlimited! However, enough of this flight of fancy; time for a reality check!

The element missing in physical cloning is the work of the Holy Spirit. Therefore, it is very doubtful that, if it is possible to clone Jesus, He would never have the spiritual powers the real Jesus had.

It is imperative that we take into consideration the issue of spiritual cloning. Recall Simon the Sorcerer in Acts 8:9–24; when he saw Peter and John place their hands on believers and they received the Holy Spirit. This is basically spiritual cloning and Simon wanted to buy this power (technology): *"Peter answered: 'May your money perish with you, because you thought you could buy the gift of God with money.'"* Many have had the ambition of spiritual cloning down through the ages; this has started many of the cults we have today. Satan is involved in this also, he is delighted to clone people in his spiritual image and many are his followers. Be careful which spiritual source is chosen for cloning!

How can we believe in spiritual cloning when there is nothing physical involved? There are, however, changes which are manifested in the physical realm. We can observe them. The fruits of The Spirit are, *"love, joy, peace, patience, kindness, goodness, faithfulness, gentleness and self-control."* (Galatians 5:22). But the fruits of the fallen nature are pride, greed, lust, hate, envy, deceit and selfishness. We would especially see this demonstrated clearly if we knew someone before and after receiving God's spiritual cloning.

Consider the process of evangelism, basically the promotion of spiritual cloning. We all want to see changes, changes that improve our being. Witnessing of spiritual cloning given in personal testimony is very powerful sales force. "You, too, can have this great change in your life! And best of all it is FREE; a gift from God." The way I see it, many are trying to cash in on this free gift, especially portrayed by classic TV evangelists. They should heed Peter's warning.

To rephrase John Kennedy's saying, "It is not what God can do for you, but what you can do for God." That is the real issue behind spiritual cloning. Spiritual cloning may be free, but there is a purpose and goal behind God's gift. It is to become His children. As His children, we must be responsive to and responsible for His call on our life. We give up all of ourselves to receive God's free gift of spiritual cloning. We are empowered to become like Jesus Christ, God's Son.

The whole story in the Bible—the work of God the Father, God the Son and God the Holy Spirit, is about our spiritual cloning to become children of God. This is found in the creation of the universe. This shows in the fallen nature of mankind through out the ages. God's Son, Jesus, coming to earth, His death on the cross and His resurrection are all part of the spiritual cloning for those chosen by God. But many are tempted by Satan to be cloned in his spiritual nature and thus lose all of eternity in Heaven; a bit of pleasure today for tomorrow we die. Be careful which spiritual cloning we choose, our eternal destiny is dependent upon that.

As a footnote, one may consider the sacraments of wine—symbolic of Christ's blood, and bread—symbolic of Christ's body, to be a symbolic form of cloning. We are being transformed into the likeness of Christ.

LINEAR AND NONLINEAR THINKING ●●●●●●●●●●●

The differences between linear and nonlinear thinking may not be intuitively obvious. Most people use linear thinking; only a very few consider nonlinear reactions. Even the classical sciences use linear thinking. The basic concept is that any complex system can be subdivided into a series or network of linear elements. The actions and reactions of these subsystems are also linear and only have linear interactions with other elements in the system.

Consider, for example, putting water in a bucket; the more water you put in the bucket, the heavier it is. That is a linear model. In a nonlinear model, as we put water in the bucket, at some point the water begins to leak out or it becomes unstable and tips over. Furthermore, below freezing water is a solid, between freezing and boiling it is a liquid, and above boiling it is a gas. At each of these transitions, we have a nonlinear region. In between these points, the behavior is generally linear. The term "linear" need not imply a linear mathematical relationship, but a relationship which has no points of nonlinearity or discontinuity over the defined region.

There is another general classification of linear thinking. This is, an action by someone or something may have only local significance and that the higher order effects are so small as to be neglected in the general scheme of things. Consider the case where we run in one direction expending energy for a short duration. The change in the worldwide wind patterns and the orbit and rotation of the earth can be neglected for all practical considerations, it is infinitesimal.

In fact, there is a very significant long-term effect. From Quantum Mechanical and Chaos Theory considerations, these are all significant events which will change the course of our earth over billions of years and may make the difference between being hit by an asteroid or not. This latter approach is also considered nonlinear. There is no such thing as an insignificant event; events can potentially couple to create major changes. Nonlinearities are a major problem in weather predictions, for example.

So what! What difference does it make? And who cares? As long as our linear thinking model works there are no problems. For almost all things we are concerned about, our linear models work. We must also consider that everyone around us communicates using linear thinking. When we come to nonlinear thinking, we stop short and have to work at it. Initially, nonlinear thinking does not make any sense; it is not what we are used to. It also makes thinking and communicating more difficult. However, the universe, the world, and people around us are all nonlinear entities. Even God is nonlinear; to understand God, we must be prepared for nonlinear thinking and understanding.

When we remain in the linear thinking domain, it is easy and natural to believe we know it all. After all, everything is but a linear extension of our experiences and what we know. If everything is linear, then, there is nothing new under the sun. There are no surprises, no funny happenings, and no spectacular events because linearity does not allow for them. Everything is perfectly predictable... and boring. Who would want to live in a linear world? There are times of over-stress when a little boring would be nice, but in general, it would not be desirable.

Perhaps the reason we have so much difficulty under-standing and accepting God is because He is so nonlinear. For one point, He is not visible; for a second, He is not limited by the physical laws that hold us captive; for a third, He does not change—He was the same before the universe came into existence and will be the same after it all passes away. Those are inconceivable in our linear thinking; they cannot exist. Furthermore, He caused the Bible to be written; not an ordinary linear book, but a nonlinear living book with power in its word. It can speak to us beyond the written words. That is unlike any other book we know. Yes, some have emotional impact, some have informational impact, and some even have life-changing impact; but the Bible is more than all these, it has the power, knowledge and wisdom of God behind them. Is this linear or nonlinear reality? Most definitely a nonlinear thinking model.

THINKING RELATIVISTICALLY ··············

Most of the time we view time and space from a linear, Newtonian perspective. That is, everyone is in agreement and obtains the same values when measuring time and space. It does not matter when or where we take our observations, all the answers come out the same. This is how we live each day. We expect it, we count on it and we cannot believe it possible to be any different. Our system would fall apart if everyone's clocks ran at a different speed and everyone's tape measure give a different answer when measuring space. It is hard enough just dealing with time zones and daylight saving time along with the conversion from feet to meters or vice versa— these are only linear corrections. Yet nonlinear time and space can and do exist!

This was first discovered by Albert Einstein in his Special Theory on Relativity in 1905, followed by his General Theory of Relativity in 1916. I find it very interesting that experiments are still being conducted today to verify all the predictions from these theories. With satellites, whole new arrays of measurements have be made. So far, all these observations continue to support Einstein's theories; now they are considered basic principles of our universe. The obvious question is, "So what?" They may be fine for scientists in their laboratory, but what difference does it make in our day-to-day lives?

Would we even recognize when we should be thinking nonlinearly and relativistically? I seriously doubt it would raise to the level of our consciousness. However, consider the creation of our universe, our world, and ourselves. The best scientific estimates now give the age of our universe at thirteen to fifteen billion years. These are from measurements taken place from our earth at the present time and from where we are in space. This general time frame has been confirmed by at least four to six different types of measurements, using different techniques and scientific principles. When we read the Bible, the common interpretation and teaching is that creation took place in six days. On such grounds, the Bible has been declared to be in total error and thus meaningless—it could not possibly have happened that way! Some have "worked" around this dilemma by saying the word "day" in Hebrew can also be interpreted as a period of time, thus exactly six periods of twenty-four hours need not be implied for creation. Others have noted that "night and day" did not exist until the earth was formed and settled down to a stable orbit; before this, a day was undefined. The assumption is that the earth is the reference point for which this was written.

The basic question relates to where the observer was when these time estimates were made. Our earth is about five billion years old as measured on the earth, so that would not be a credible reference point when going all the way back to the beginning of creation, which is now believed to have started at an infinitesimally small point. If we assume Heaven was God's viewpoint, which would be outside this expanding universe, and our viewpoint is from inside this expanding universe, we can make some calculations. The equation is relatively simple; $(T_2-T_1)=(t_2-t_1) \times (1-(v^2/c^2))^{0.5}$, where "T" is time outside the universe and "t" is the time inside the expanding universe. So, if we use the outside time difference as six days and the inside time difference at 13 billion years, all we have to do is solve for "v", the velocity inside our expanding universe. And, "c," of course, is the velocity of light. Now it should be noted that this is the more simple Special Theory of Relativity and does not include any gravitational effects that come into play, given in the General Theory of Relativity, which most certainly would have their effects on the calculations (but are also unknown in any detail for inside the universe). The answer is, the average expansion velocity equals 0.9999999999999999996 the velocity of light—a result we really expected beforehand, as the universe is still rapidly expanding.

The main point to be made from this development is that with nonlinear thinking, by using the Special Theory of Relativity we find that six days can equal thirteen billion years, just depending upon from where one views creation. Thus, there may be other explanations when we come to an impasse between science and the Bible. It should also be noted that, after the time of Adam and Eve, the reference point of the Bible does shift to earth, and there is general agreement between science and the Bible for the dates of other events given in the Old and New Testament.

THE HIDDEN WORLDS AROUND US ·············

Could it possibly be there are great vast regions around us we cannot see? The answer to this is a very strong, "YES." How can this be? For today's understanding of physics, there is no explanation. What is observed is the effects of mass in the very large regions of space. How large might these be? Vast and beyond our imagination! In the last ten years there have been major advances in astronomy and cosmology. The best estimates at present are that all the stars and galaxies we see in our universe amounts for roughly 0.5 percent of the total mass in our universe! That is, we see only 1/200th of what is really out there! Taking into account the invisible clouds of atoms, this number increases to only five percent of the mass. The rest is cold dark matter and dark energy. Although astronomers cannot see this cold dark matter directly, they know it accounts for about thirty percent of the matter in the universe because of the ways it pulls on stars and bends light. This dark matter contains sixty times as much mass as the mass we do see. The dark matter is believed to be congealed into filaments that thread the surfaces of cosmic voids hundreds to millions of light-years across. Because of the weak interaction of the cold dark mass with the mass we see, there is a different physics force involved; not the tradi-tional four major forces of gravity, electro-magnetic force, and weak and strong nuclear forces. We have sixty-five per-cent of total density of the universe in dark energy remaining. So far the best that can be done is name it. It has the charac-teristics of repulsive force like anti-gravity. To explain the var-ious forces and interactions, physicists are now using eleven-dimensional time-spacial coordinates, far beyond our familiar three dimensions of space. Can all this be real? Just as real as the physical measurements of our visible world!

There is another hidden world around us that is also getting little attention. This the the spiritual world. It does not use the physical dimensions of space and time, which throws our logic and understanding out of sync. We have great difficulty imagining or comprehending a world that is nonphysical. Therefore we must use other dimensions such as power, majesty, knowledge, wisdom, emotions, basic nature, relationships and communications. These are mostly nonphysical, with some reservations about power and communications.

What kind of power and communications are we dealing with if they are nonphysical? Is it possible to have nonphysical dimensions that interact with the physical dimensions? The answer must be yes, because God, a spirit, created the universe, the world and all living things from His spiritual domain. Therefore, the spiritual world must be greater than the physical world.

If there are interactions between the spiritual and physical worlds, they should be observable by us. It is doubtful that these interactions would be as obvious as the laws of physics, because our physical laws have no coupling with the spiritual world. In developing these physical laws we have specifically rejected any possibility of interactions with the spiritual world. Thus, any observable interaction between the spiritual and physical worlds would not follow the conditions of our physical laws. From a scientific point of view, they are unobservable. However, from an emotional, consciousness or feelings domain, these interactions should be quite observable. These are nonphysical interactions. Looking for these interactions in some organized way should be profitable. The various religions represent a starting point, but all seems confusing because of the many beliefs and views of the spiritual domain. For me, the Christian theology presents the most clean and logical position.

The above rather long summary of present cosmic technology and a postulation of the spiritual world is provided for comparison. Interestingly, we find vast areas in our physical universe which are beyond our present understanding and are completely mystifying. What we actually see is only 0.5 percent of what is really there. Now, considering our spiritual world, we could easily conclude that, again, what we actually observe indirectly is perhaps 0.5 percent of what is really there.

So what is our problem? How can we accept the physical world and not the spiritual world when we see both only in part, and a very small part at that? If we find the very small part of the stars, galaxies and nebula so exciting, why should we not also find God, who created these wonders also very exciting? Do we need to know everything before saying we believe? This does not seem to be the case in the physical world, so why the bias towards the spiritual world? God's Word in the Bible is a very good place to start in understanding the spiritual world.

ANTHROPOMORPHIC THEORETICAL PHYSICS

We all have problems in relating to the four force fields in physics. Therefore, let us try to relate these force fields in an analogous way to human functions and forces. Let us take an anthropomorphic view of Theoretical Physics. A few of us may want to give up at this point, but I would encourage continuing on for just a bit, as it might produce some interesting correlations.

The four force fields in physics are electromagnetic, gravitational, and weak and strong nuclear forces. The electromagnetic forces include electro-static, magnetic, and the wide electromagnetic spectrum from radio waves to gamma and cosmic rays. I am relating this very broad force field to the command, control and sense functions of the brain—its memory, logic, intuition, conscious and automatic control of our body. It is the driving force keeping us moving and functioning each day.

For the gravitational force, I have chosen to relate this to the sexual responses and the attraction force of two bodies. The gravitational force is inversely proportional to distance; the closer the two bodies, the stronger the force. The gravitational force is also similar in that it is directly related to the size and form of the bodies and sexual exposure. Certainly Freud should agree that sex is one of the dominate forces in humans sociology.

Now, on to the strong and weak nuclear forces. This comparison is a little more difficult as these forces are generally smaller and operate at very short distances. Thus, I have chosen the emotions for the strong force and the subconscious for the weak force; they are our internal forces.

The next step is to relate these human forces to the three major general theories in physics: the General Theory of Relativity of Einstein (the macroscopic), the Quantum Mechanical Field Theory of Planck, Dirack, Pauli, Schwinger, Feynman and others (the microscopic), and the integrating Superstring Theory of Veneziano, using Euler's earlier mathematical developments and further development by Nambu, Nielsen, Susskind and many others to provide the synergistic combination of both Relativity and Quantum theories.

We may thus choose to combine the intellectual and sexual forces into the Relativistic Theory and the emotions and subconscious forces into the Quantum Theory. This leaves the Superstring Theory to pull these two forces together, just as it does in the physical world.

We have just covered some physical aspects of human life. What about our spiritual life? How might we compare or relate that? A new challenge, but we shall fearlessly charge ahead. In the spiritual domain we can consider how God created the heavens, the earth, living plants, animals and stuff, and then humans. We can relate the plants and animals to the electromagnetic force, the humans to the gravitational force, the earth to the strong nuclear force and the heavens to the weak nuclear forces. This is a bit arbitrary, but the plants and animals represent a broad spectrum of life needed to support the ecosystem. Certainly the humans try to pull everything together and exert control, as gravity does. The earth is a general strong nucleus holding us together, and the heavens, being far, far away, are a very weak force as far as directly affecting our lives.

Now on to the next step, "What about God?" This perhaps is a bit easier. God the Father would represent the

General Theory of Relativity. God the Holy Spirit would represent the Quantum Mechanics Field Theory, and God the Son, as our Lord and Saviour, is the Superstring Theory, involved in bringing everything together.

So, what do we make of this game? Perhaps we are going at this all backwards by taking our model of the physical world and using it to interpret the living world and then the spiritual world. The order of creation was the reverse of this. God, pre-existing, created the spiritual beings and kingdoms, then prepared a physical universe suitable for the living plants and animals, and continued on to the creation of humankind in His image. The problem is God did not directly give us a full set of physical laws. We have had to dig them out ourselves—probably with His help and guidance. Since God created the physical world, we would expect that His nature is related. Thus, though being a bit arbitrary, it still may not be all that far off as a consideration and starting point.

DEFYING RATIONALITY, YET PROVIDING ANSWERS ················

At a recent economic conference, George Schultz related a conversation he had with Mikhail Gorbachev on supply-and-demand economics. Gorbachev just could not understand such a concept, a concept that defies rational control, yet provides answers. How can this be?

First we need to understand supply-and-demand economics. The basic concept is the government does nothing; they stay out of price-fixing, entitlements, rationing, bail-outs, tax incentives, and all other sorts of rules and regulations. It is a process that lets the market work freely in adjusting the price and supply to balance the demand of consumers.

For example, assume the demand for a given product increases. If the capacity to meet the increased demand is available, there is little incentive to raise the prices. However, if the capacity is not available, the price increases to a value where the supply equals the demand. As the price increases, there is an incentive for the suppliers to increase production which generally requires additional costs. As the cost increase, the consumer will find alternate approaches, different suppliers, or conserve usage to satisfy their demand. If the government comes in with controls, this natural process is interrupted. Price-freezes provide no incentive for suppliers to increase production or for consumers to conserve or find alternate approaches. Also, it is generally not possible to predict when there will be changes in the supplies or demands; they just happen.

When we experience very hot weather, the demand for electricity rises to peak levels during the day but drops back to normal in the evenings, nights and mornings. These excursions can be a factor of 100 times. To meet these peak demands requires generating plants that are idle most of the time and are therefore very inefficient to run, with the cost of generation also about ten times the baseline cost of power.

On the other side of the curve, as demand drops, supply also must drop. The more efficient companies can lower their price and capture a larger portion of the market. If this lasts more than a short period, the less efficient companies will go out of business, or change their product and market. If the government goes in with bail-out funds, this keeps the inefficient companies in business and all incentives for improvements and efficiency are lost, even for the companies that are doing well.

Politically there is great pressure for government to enter the marketplace, control the process and, in many countries, take over the industry. In this way, it is assumed that everyone will be satisfied. Generally, government-run systems are not profitable, very inefficient, do not change to meet changing conditions and if they do change, it is a very slow process. There are no incentives to be efficient, improve products, or let the competitive process work. There is great fear in the government when they are not in control. This was Gorbachev's problem. He has been in government all his life and has never seen competition in supply-and-demand economics work. He could not conceive of such a system being more efficiently and effectively run than a government-run system.

In a free economy, there are great risks and great rewards for companies. Those who error in supplying the market will not be in business very long. For those who get it right, there are great rewards. Many consider this an unfair system. The people in companies that failed worked just as hard as those whose companies achieve great success. Therefore something should be done to remove the great swings in risk and rewards. The free market system seems unfair to many.

Consider God's "economy." There is great range of successes and failures. Natural disasters strike some but not others. Some people are more genetically endowed and thus more able to do things then others. Those who accept Jesus Christ as the Lord and Saviour will have eternal life in Heaven with God and those who do not, will be cast to the outermost regions of torment.

Many evaluating God's actions and what He allows to happen, claim, "God is unfair!" Even God runs a supply-and-demand system; Scriptures note, *"Ask and it will be given to you; seek and you will find; knock and the door will be opened to you."* (Matthew 7:7). God has an infinite supply of help and answers but we have a low demand, which is why the cost is low; we try to do everything ourselves rather than turn to God in faith and submission asking Him in prayer for help. On the other hand, salvation comes at a very high price: the admission of our sins, the change of our lifestyles and acceptance of Jesus as our Lord and Master; thus the demand is very low.

....

CHAPTER 5

Playing with Words on Purpose

The English language permits a wide range of games to be played with words. It is occasionally relaxing to write a short piece untangling the various meanings and spellings of words. The theme of all of these is still a focus on God.

> For some extraordinary reason, the Church moves in an atmosphere of antiquity. I have no doubt that it makes for dignity; I have also no doubt that there are times when it makes for complete irrelevance; for, if there is one thing that is true of religion it is that it must always be expressible in contemporary terms. Religion fails if it cannot speak to men as they are.
>
> William Barclay (1907–1978), *In the Hands of God*

Where there is fear of God to keep the house, the enemy can find no way to enter.

Francis of Assisi (1182–1226)

HEMATOLOGICAL RELATIONSHIPS ··············

Many people do not like using the word, "blood," or talking about blood. It just sends shivers through their body. I must admit I do not like looking at blood, or talking about it, either. This is in part from having a rock hit me in the face when I was at school and running to the school nurse with blood all over, and in part from having nosebleeds during my younger years. There is something mysterious and threatening about blood. It is a lifeforce that gives us existence. Early civilizations believed that all life was in the blood. Obviously, if the blood is removed, life quickly ends. In light of the general discomfort, I have chosen to use the medical term "hematology" as the title for discussing this issue.

Genealogy is the study of hematological relationships. We start out with our parents, and search back to their parents and other brothers and sisters. Then, there are all the marriages of the children from various generations, which spread out our hematological relationship tree. I often wonder how far back we can trace our relationships. If we are very diligent, resourceful, and experience a good portion of coincidences, we can end up back to Adam and Eve, the first two humans on earth. Thus, by that association, everyone on earth is hematologically-related, it is just a matter of the distance of the relationship.

When we consider family, we normally include only the immediate members. These numbers reach astronomical proportions if we are to include everyone; this becomes impractical in a four-dimensional space and time. At best, we could get to know twenty-five people in great detail. As the number increases, the relationships dwindle to only acquaintances and name recognition. As the group gets smaller, we are able to know the members more intimately in all of life's trials and triumphs. It is a joy to share our life's walk (or run if you are able) with other close members. There is usually much in common in close hematological relationships; we are therefore also close genetically which implies similar interests, attitudes and personalities most of the time; of course, there are the exceptions.

There is another significant hematological relationship and that is our health history and prospects. Many predisposed health conditions are related to family members. This type of information is one of the most important, requested to update individual health records and for increased monitoring of potential genetic disorders.

The genetic history follows our hematological relationships, nothing really new. Unfortunately, there has seldom been a careful documentation by family members of health issues in genealogical relationships. This is rapidly changing. As our knowledge of genetic relationships to medical history develops, perhaps then the medical history of our parents will not be so important.

In the Old Testament, the Mosaic Laws carefully connected hematological relationships with specific sins; that is, they performed hematological sacrifices of specific animals. This ritual was meticulously carried out by the temple priests at the sacrificial altar. During high religious days, it was even said a hematology river flowed from the Temple. Hematological sprinkling over those who sought forgiveness of sin was also part of the ritual. In part, this was all symbolic of things to come.

All of this hematological sacrifice was looking forward to the New Testament times with the coming of Jesus, the perfect sin offering where on the cross His hematological offering was an accepted payment in full of the sins for all those who repented and followed Jesus Christ as their Lord and Saviour. To confirm the acceptance of Jesus' sacrificial offering, God His Father resurrected Him back to life to appear to His apostles and shortly thereafter, Jesus return to Heaven.

There is great power in Jesus' hematological sacrifice. We do not fully understand the full depth of this sacrifice. We only guess at the hematological significance and its symbolic nature. In a physiological description, the hematological actions bring energy and nutrients to all the cells of our body and then also remove all the waste and foreign products, transporting them to the kidneys,—to only name two functions. This may also be symbolic of Jesus' spiritual work of salvation and sanctification—removing our sins and transgressions along with bringing us energy, guidance and wholeness.

I BELIEVE I BELIEVE WHAT I BELIEVE ···········

If I see it with my own eyes, then I will believe! If you show me how it is done, then I will believe. If God said it, then I will believe. So go a long list of things I really do believe I believe! There are occasional problems; I do not always believe what I believe. How can that be? I believe the problem is with our use of "believe;" the word has an absolute, relative and abstract conditional meaning. All beliefs are not the same! Let us consider some examples:

I believe my car will start this morning. Then I go out to start my car and it does not start. Is there something wrong with my belief? Similarly, I believe my wristwatch has the right time. So I go to a meeting and find I am twenty-five minutes late. What happened? Or, I believe the Bible is the Word of God; a true and absolute guide for my life. Then someone points to a specific passage in the Bible and asks, "Do you really believe this?" Now I have a problem, because I cannot say I really believe that one specific passage.

The problem is not in my belief, but in my use of the word "believe"—it does not mean the same thing in each case. My thesaurus gives the synonyms: "accept, hold, maintain, presume, know, have faith, swear by, give credence to, trust, suspect, take as gospel, suppose, assume, guess, and surmise." These span the range from "guess" to "swear by"! So then we should rewrite the title of this essay as, "I guess I give credence to what I suspect" or, "I have faith that I hold to what I know." Now, is that any better? Both are really saying the same thing, "I believe I believe what I believe." This being the case, "What difference does it make what I believe?" Is it just the same whatever we believe? Not according to the Scriptures.

The disciple John wrote:

Jesus did many other miraculous signs in the presence of his disciples, which are not recorded in this book. But these are written that you may believe that Jesus is the Christ, the Son of God, and that by believing you may have life in his name (John 20:30–31).

"Salvation is found in no one else, for there is no other name under heaven given to men by which we must be saved" (Acts 4:12). What must we believe to be saved for eternal life?

Jesus said, *"If you believe, you will receive whatever you ask for in prayer"* (Matthew 21:22).

"O unbelieving generation," Jesus replied, "how long shall I stay with you? How long shall I put up with you? Bring the boy to me." Jesus asked the boy's father, "How long has he been like this?" "From childhood," he answered, ...But if you can do anything, take pity on us and help us." "'If you can'?" said Jesus, "Everything is possible for him who believes." Immediately the boy's father exclaimed, "I do believe, help me overcome my unbelief!" (Mark 9:19,21–24).

We all need this help when facing impossible conditions. Does it make any difference what we believe? I believe the universe is fifteen billion years old but others believe it is only a few tens of thousands of years. It does affect interpretations of early history, but generally there is little affect on our lives.

On the other hand, I believe trains are dangerous and am careful at railroad crossings. Some do not; typically there are several hundred deaths per year at railroad crossings—people taking chances.

Then there is our belief in God and the saving power of believing in Jesus Christ. Our eternity is dependent upon what we believe and in whom we put our faith. I believe this is very important and spend a lot of time getting to know God, and thanking Him for all He does in my life. I believe I will spend eternity with God in Heaven. Many do not believe in God; they consider all religions a waste of time. Still others are out pursuing false religions, which have no power behind them other than the belief of other believers.

It is all a matter of how strongly we follow our beliefs and how true our beliefs are. "I believe I believe what I believe" can imply many different things, but it is the way we live our lives that truly reveals what we believe. If we say we believe, but do not live our beliefs, our beliefs have little value. Yet if our beliefs really shape our lives, then our beliefs have meaning.

For example, my cardiologist says I have a bad heart. I somewhat believe him. However, when my heart goes through angina pain, I am a real believer that I have a bad heart. I am reminded daily by gentle restrictions in my heart performance and about once a month by some serious pain. My heart is constantly maintaining the strength of my belief, and it makes all the difference imaginable in my lifestyle. If there is something I can do to help my heart, I am doing it!

I believe it is the same way with God. We all have a serious condition called "sin." We are reminded daily of our sinful nature. If we respond to God's love and repent, God will forgive our sins and heal us. There is great joy, peace and love as we believe in God and follow His direction for our lives.

AYE, I EYE! ••••••••••••••

Aye, I eye, or yes, I see! But do we all eye the same? Aye or Nay? Do we recognize and understand everything comes in our eyes? The natural assumptions is, "Of course!" We make most of our judgments in life through our eyes; if we can just see it, then all will be understood and believed. Seeing is more important than hearing. What we see, we believe. Hearing can have doubts. If some one tells us or we read it, that is really second hand. Consider,

> *Later Jesus appeared to the Eleven as they were eating; he rebuked them for their lack of faith and their stubborn refusal to believe those who had seen him after he had risen* (Mark 15:14).

To a very large extent, we do not recognize or understand what we see! For example, when we look at a red ball, what do our eyes see? An object round in shape and red in color. First, it is red because all the other colors are absorbed by the surface material and red is the only color not absorbed, but reflected. This assumes a white light is shining on the ball. If a green-blue light were shining on the ball it would appear black in color. Next, the object is round, at least in the two dimensions we see from the direction we are looking. This does not tell us if it is heavy or light, hard or soft, inflated or deflated or if it could bounce like a ball. These all must be determined by other than just looking. Also, the image could be projected on a screen or a hologram, and not a real object at all.

A similar point can be made looking at the stars in the heavens. They are points of light, but just by using our eyes, we cannot tell how far they are away or how big they are, or what their composition is. I propose that we understand far less than half of what we see with our eyes, but hardly ever take that into consideration when we say, "Aye, I eye," implying we fully understand. Why is this?

Other conditions come upon us as the years add up. I cannot find things I am looking for because I do not recognize them even when I looking directly at them. Somehow the size, shape, and texture of what I want to find are not recognized in the field of view of my eyes. I eye, but I don't eye them, aye! What might be the cause for this condition?

> *He [Jesus] replied, "The knowledge of the secrets of the kingdom of heaven has been given to you, but not to them. Whoever does not have, even what he has will be taken from him." This is why I speak to them in parables: "Though seeing, they do not see; though hearing, they do not hear or understand." In them is fulfilled the prophecy of Isaiah: "You will be ever hearing but never understanding; you will be ever seeing but never perceiving. For this people's heart has become calloused; they hardly hear with their ears, and they have closed their eyes. Otherwise they might see with their eyes, hear with their ears, understand with their hearts and turn, and I would heal them"* (Matthew 13:13–15).

There are a number of factors going on here. The eyes are faithful sensors most of the time, but the optical processing and recognition is subject to preconditioning, expected patterns, and the lack of full knowledge and wisdom about understanding what we are looking at. We normally operate in a preconceived adapted environment and anticipate what we should be "seeing." If what we "see" is not in line with our beliefs, we normally will not see it, and vice versa. Or if we expect to see something, we may see that even though it may not truly exist in our field of view. An example is the case of witnesses of an accident—they all have different stories.

There are a number of "visual" anomalies we seldom consider. First, we are blind in the area where the optical nerve comes into our eye. For the right eye, it is off to the right about mid-height and for the left, off to the left. These voids in our seeing are not recognized. Second, our visual acuity is greatest in the center section of our eye and resolution degrades towards the edges—also generally not noticed. There are a number of other anomalies which generally have little effect.

Now on the the spiritual considerations. Not only is the Holy Spirit at work for those who are close to God providing additional insight, but also Satan, the great deceiver, is at work trying to inhibit any recognition of God's existence or His works. These influences can significantly affect our ability to recognize and understand what we see. As we age, all these processes become more degraded and slower. Aye, I see, but, *"Now we see but a poor reflection as in a mirror"* (1 Corinthians 13:12).

SENT CENTS FOR SENSE FROM SCENTS ········

There are times when I have real serious problem in following a trail of scents. Like a dog with its nose to the ground, I follow the paths of life, making decisions at each juncture point. Often I make the wrong decisions and have to backtrack, sometimes at great expense. If I had just spent a few cents for some common sense I would have saved myself a lot of trouble, not following the wrong scents. Quite often, as we follow the scents, we do not know where they will lead. It is only after we get there that everything becomes clear. If there were just a way to acquire sense, I would be willing to have sent some cents to do that. Just how might this all work?

For example, I first bought a big telescope; it worked great and I have a lot of good images of deep space objects. However, the telescope is really not portable. In the summer we go off to our mountain cabin, over which there are usually nice, dark skies—great for astronomy—but I previously needed a more portable system. So I did some research into the subject of small scopes, and a friend recommended a used six-inch Newtonian, was designed for photography. I followed the scents. That sounded like all I needed and was about half the weight and half the size. I was all excited when it came, but for a year and a half now, I have yet to take a good image from this telescope. It has been one problem after another. I am still trying to figure out what is going wrong and have spent a few cents calling around to telescope optical professions. As of today, no success to report. I have gone so far as to put up sale scents so someone else with more sense can figure out how to get it to work for less cents than I paid for it.

There is another area on the path of life where we often follow the wrong scent; that is in religion. The great deceiver, Satan, is out putting false and misleading scents along the path to God. The question here is, "where can we spend a few cents to find some good sense not to follow the wrong scents and end up being sent to Hell? There is a good handbook for a few cents that will give us common sense so we can follow the right scent from God. It is the Bible, God's Words of Wisdom sent to us. Everyone should have sent cents for sense from scents leading to God, salvation and eternal life. Satan uses the strongest scents he can find to lead us astray. Sometimes these scents are so strong they override our good sense and have sent us on dead-end trails that cost a lot of cents.

Some may ask, "Why, if God created us, did he not spend a few more cents on better sense to follow His scent?" That is enmeshed in the difference between beings with no free will and those who do have it. To have free will includes being able to reject our Creator, and many do. They want to be their own creator, and they have the free will to do that. They will pay a very high price for this rebellion from God and His will for their lives. Consider the angels, spiritual beings far more powerful and capable than ourselves. One third of the angels left God in order to follow Satan and his rebellion, to make themselves higher than God. If they can reject God with their higher sense, we have no basis to complain.

There are coming events, the end of time and the judgment day, when we all will be evaluated on how we have used our cents, our sense and our scents that God has sent us. Those who have not used God's resources successfully will be will be condemned. All is not lost for those who had the good sense to follow Jesus Christ as the Lord and Master and have followed the life path scents He has given them; they will be saved, as Jesus Christ has paid our penalty. We need to continuously send our spiritual prayer cents to God for His good sense so that we may follow the true scent of life. Thus we have stored in Heaven our rewards for the good use of our cents and our sense from all the scents God has sent us.

•••••••••••••••••••••••••••••

Index of Writings

Endnotes

Section Quotations—online

Adams, Robert McAnully, Curator
Christian Quote of the Day
<http://www.gospelcom.net/cqod>
Forward Micklem—Jan 16, 2002
Introduction Aquinas—Jan 28, 2002

Chapter 1 Jones—Jan 7, 2002

Chapter 2 Alexander—Jan 5, 2002

Chapter 3 Law—Dec 1, 2001

Chapter 4 Pascal—Jan 5, 2002

Chapter 5 Barclay—Jan 9, 2002 & Assisi—Oct 4, 2001

Chapter 4 quotes of Einstein & Barrow from e-mail of Angela Boren,
    Jan, 2002